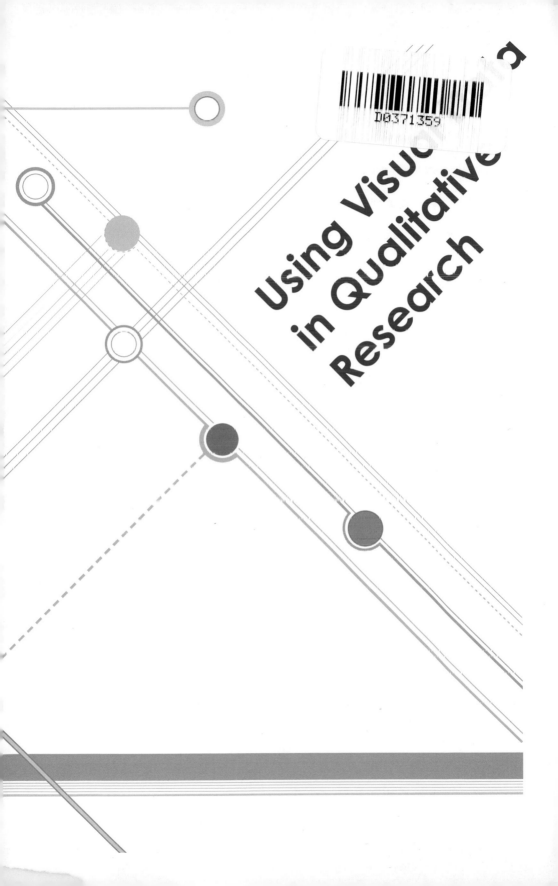

Using Visual Data
in Qualitative
Research

Using Visual Data in Qualitative Research (by Marcus Banks) is the fifth part of *The SAGE Qualitative Research Kit*. This *Kit* comprises eight books and taken together the *Kit* represents the most extensive and detailed introduction to the process of doing qualitative research. This book can be used in conjunction with other titles in the *Kit* as part of this overall introduction to qualitative methods but this book can equally well be used on its own as an introduction to the use of visual data in qualitative research.

Complete list of titles in *The SAGE Qualitative Research Kit*

- Designing Qualitative Research *Uwe Flick*
- Doing Interviews *Steinar Kvale*
- Doing Ethnographic and Observational Research *Michael Angrosino*
- Doing Focus Groups *Rosaline Barbour*
- Using Visual Data in Qualitative Research *Marcus Banks*
- Analysing Qualitative Data *Graham R. Gibbs*
- Doing Conversation, Discourse and Document Analysis *Tim Rapley*
- Managing Quality in Qualitative Research *Uwe Flick*

Members of the Editorial Advisory Board

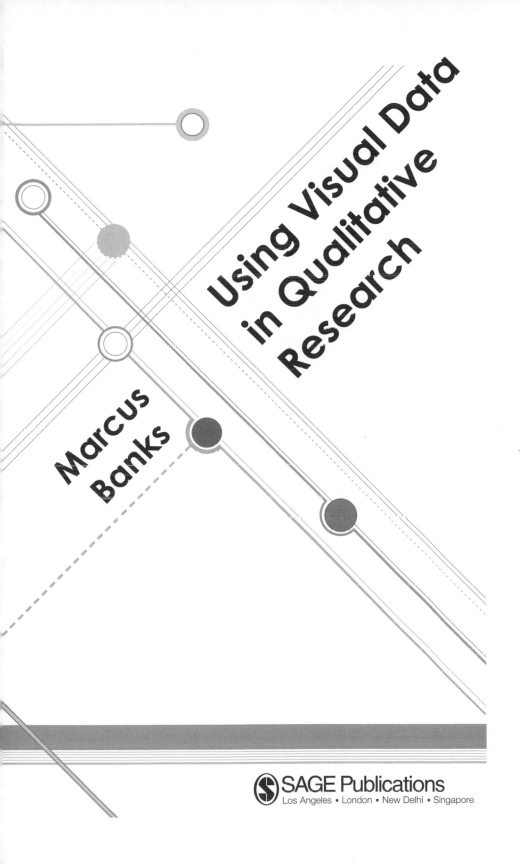

Using Visual Data in Qualitative Research

Marcus Banks

SAGE Publications
Los Angeles · London · New Delhi · Singapore

First published 2007

SAGE Publications Ltd
1 Oliver's Yard
55 City Road
London EC1Y 1SP

SAGE Publications Inc.
2455 Teller Road
Thousand Oaks, California 91320

SAGE Publications India Pvt Ltd
B 1/I 1 Mohan Cooperative Industrial Area
Mathura Road, New Delhi 110 044
India

SAGE Publications Asia-Pacific Pte Ltd
33 Pekin Street #02-01
Far East Square
Singapore 048763

Library of Congress Control Number 2006938287

British Library Cataloguing in Publication data

A catalogue record for this book is available from the British Library

ISBN 978-0-7619-4979-4

Typeset by C&M Digitals (P) Ltd, Chennai, India
Printed in Great Britain by The Cromwell Press Ltd, Trowbridge, Wiltshire
Printed on paper from sustainable resources

▐▐▐ Contents

III List of illustrations

Boxes

Figures

Editorial introduction
Uwe Flick

- Introduction to *The SAGE Qualitative Research Kit*
- What is qualitative research?
- How do we conduct qualitative research?
- Scope of *The SAGE Qualitative Research Kit*

Introduction to *The SAGE Qualitative Research Kit*

In recent years, qualitative research has enjoyed a period of unprecedented growth and diversification as it has become an established and respected research approach across a variety of disciplines and contexts. An increasing number of students, teachers and practitioners are facing questions and problems of how to do qualitative research – in general and for their specific individual purposes. To answer these questions, and to address such practical problems on a how-to-do level, is the main purpose of *The SAGE Qualitative Research Kit*.

The books in *The SAGE Qualitative Research Kit* collectively address the core issues that arise when we actually do qualitative research. Each book focuses on key methods (e.g. interviews or focus groups) or materials (e.g. visual data or discourse) that are used for studying the social world in qualitative terms. Moreover, the books in the *Kit* have been written with the needs of many different types of reader in mind. As such, the *Kit* and the individual books will be of use to a wide variety of users:

- *Practitioners* of qualitative research in the social sciences, medical research, marketing research, evaluation, organizational, business and management studies, cognitive science, etc., who face the problem of planning and conducting a specific study using qualitative methods.
- *University teachers* and lecturers in these fields using qualitative methods will be expected to use these series as a basis of their teaching.

- *Undergraduate and graduate students* of social sciences, nursing, education, psychology and other fields where qualitative methods are a (main) part of the university training including practical applications (e.g. for writing a thesis).

Each book in *The SAGE Qualitative Research Kit* has been written by a distinguished author with extensive experience in their field and practised in with methods they write about. When reading the whole series of books from the beginning to the end, you will repeatedly come across some issues which are central to any sort of qualitative research – such as ethics, designing research or assessing quality. However, in each book such issues are addressed from the specific methodological angle of the authors and the approach they describe. Thus you may find different approaches to issues of quality or different suggestions of how to analyze qualitative data in the different books, which will combine to present a comprehensive picture of the field as a whole.

What is qualitative research?

It has become more and more difficult to find a common definition of qualitative research which is accepted by the majority of qualitative research approaches land researchers. Qualitative research is no longer just simply '*not* quantitative research', but has developed an identity (or maybe multiple identities) of its own.

Despite the multiplicity of approaches to qualitative research, some common features of qualitative research can be identified. Qualitative research is intended to approach the world 'out there' (not in specialized research settings such as laboratories) and to understand, describe and sometimes explain social phenomena 'from the inside' in a number of different ways:

- By analyzing experiences of individuals or groups. Experiences can be related to biographical life histories or to (everyday or professional) practices; they may be addressed by analyzing everyday knowledge, accounts and stories.
- By analyzing interactions and communications in the making. This can be based on observing or recording practices of interacting and communicating and analyzing this material.
- By analyzing documents (texts, images, film or music) or similar traces of experiences or interactions.

Common to such approaches is that they seek to unpick how people construct the world around them, what they are doing or what is happening to them in terms that are meaningful and that offer rich insight. Interactions and documents are seen as ways of constituting social processes and artefacts collaboratively (or conflictingly). All of these approaches represent ways of meaning, which can be reconstructed and analyzed with different qualitative methods that allow the researcher to develop (more or less generalizable) models, typologies, theories as ways of describing and explaining social (or psychological) issues.

How do we conduct qualitative research?

Can we identify common ways of doing qualitative research if we take into account that there are different theoretical, epistemological and methodological approaches to qualitative research and that the issues that are studied are very diverse as well? We can at least identify some common features of how qualitative research is done.

- Qualitative researchers are interested in accessing experiences, interactions and documents in their natural context and in a way that gives room to the particularities of them and the materials in which they are studied.
- Qualitative research refrains from setting up a well-defined concept of what is studied and from formulating hypotheses in the beginning in order to test them. Rather, concepts (or hypotheses, if they are used) are developed and refined in the process of research.
- Qualitative research starts from the idea that methods and theories should be appropriate to what is studied. If the existing methods do not fit to a concrete issue or field, they are adapted or new methods or approaches are developed.
- Researchers themselves are an important part of the research process, either in terms of their own personal presence as researchers, or in terms of their experiences in the field and with the reflexivity they bring to the role – as are members of the field under study.
- Qualitative research takes context and cases seriously for understanding an issue under study. A lot of qualitative research is based on case studies or a series of case studies, and often the case (its history and complexity) is an important context for understanding what is studied.
- A major part of qualitative research is based on text and writing – from field notes and transcripts to descriptions and interpretations and finally to the presentation of the findings and of the research as a whole. Therefore, issues of transforming complex social situations (or other materials such as images) into texts – issues of transcribing and writing in general – are major concerns of qualitative research.
- If methods are supposed to be adequate to what is under study, approaches to defining and assessing the quality of qualitative research (still) have to be discussed in specific ways that are appropriate for qualitative research and even for specific approaches in qualitative research.

Scope of *The SAGE Qualitative Research Kit*

- *Designing Qualitative Research* (Uwe Flick) gives a brief introduction to qualitative research from the point of view of how to plan and design a concrete study using qualitative research in one way or the other. It is intended to outline a framework for the other books in *The Sage Qualitative Research Kit* by focusing on how-to-do problems and on how to solve such problems in the research process. The book will address issues of constructing a research design in qualitative research; it will outline stepping-stones in making a research project work and will discuss practical problems such as resources in qualitative research but also more methodological issues like quality of qualitative research and also ethics. This framework is spelled out in more details in the other books in the Kit.
- Three books are devoted to collecting or producing data in qualitative research. They take up the issues briefly outlined in the first book and approach them in a much more detailed and focused way for the specific method. First, *Doing Interviews* (Steinar Kvale) addresses the theoretical, epistemological, ethical and practical issues of interviewing people about specific issues or their life history. *Doing Ethnographic and Observational Research* (Michael Angrosino) focuses on the second major approach to collecting and producing qualitative data. Here again practical issues (like selecting sites, methods of collecting data in ethnography, special problems of analyzing them) are discussed in the context of more general issues (ethics, representations, quality and adequacy of ethnography as an approach). In *Doing Focus Groups* (Rosaline Barbour) the third of the most important qualitative methods of producing data is presented. Here again we find a strong focus on how-to-do issues of sampling, designing and analyzing the data and on how to produce them in focus groups.
- Three further volumes are devoted to analyzing specific types of qualitative data. *Using Visual Data in Qualitative Research* (Marcus Banks) extends the focus to the third type of qualitative data (beyond verbal data coming from interviews and focus groups and observational data). The use of visual data has not only become a major trend in social research in general, but confronts researchers with new practical problems in using them and analyzing them and produces new ethical issues. In *Analyzing Qualitative Data* (Graham Gibbs), several practical approaches and issues of making sense of any sort of qualitative data are addressed. Special attention is paid to practices of coding, of comparing and of using computer-assisted qualitative data analysis. Here, the focus is on verbal data like interviews, focus groups or biographies. *Doing Conversation, Discourse and Document Analysis* (Tim Rapley) extends this focus to different types of data, relevant for analyzing discourses. Here, the focus is on existing material (like documents) and on recording everyday conversations and on finding traces of discourses. Practical issues such as

generating an archive, transcribing video materials and of how to analyze discourses with such types of data are discussed.

- *Managing Quality in Qualitative Research* (Uwe Flick) takes up the issue of quality in qualitative research, which has been briefly addressed in specific contexts in other books in the *Kit*, in a more general way. Here, quality is looked at from the angle of using or reformulating existing or defining new criteria for qualitative research. This book will examine the ongoing debates about what should count as defining 'quality' and validity in qualitative methodologies and will examine the many strategies for promoting and managing quality in qualitative research. Special attention is paid to the strategy of triangulation in qualitative research and to the use of quantitative research in the context of promoting the quality of qualitative research.

Before I go on to outline the focus of this book and its role in the *Kit*, I would like to thank some people at SAGE who were important in making this *Kit* happen. Michael Carmichael suggested this project to me some time ago and was very helpful with his suggestions in the beginning. Patrick Brindle took over and continued this support, as did Vanessa Harwood and Jeremy Joynsee in making books out of the manuscripts we provided.

About this book
Uwe Flick

Visual data have become a prominent approach in qualitative research in general, after they have been used for some time in areas such as visual anthropology. By focusing on this type of data, this book brings a new perspective into *The SAGE Qualitative Research Kit* as most of the discussion in the other books concentrates on the spoken word or the observation of practices. Although both books are about different forms of field research, this book's closest connection is with the one on ethnography by Angrosino (2007), although there are similar links to the one on discourse analysis by Rapley (2007), too. The latter and this book take materials for their analysis that often exist and are mainly selected and documented and not so much produced for research purposes. These materials become data mainly in the process of analyzing. Therefore, both come with a more integrated approach to data production and analysis, which takes the specific quality of the materials into account. Nevertheless, suggestions from the book of Gibbs (2007) for analyzing qualitative data may be helpful for this context also, as this book too is interested in the use of computers for the analysis of data. As visual data are sometimes used in combination with verbal data methods (in photo-elicitation techniques, for example), the books of Kvale (2007) on interviews or Barbour (2007) on focus groups may complement this book as well.

The focus of this book is on historical, theoretical and practical approaches to using visual data in qualitative research. It comes with a lot of case study material, which illustrates the approaches. It also addresses special problems of ethics in visual research and of how to present findings from using visual methods to academic and other audiences and research participants themselves.

In the core of the book we find issues of how to do a study using visual data, starting from clarifying the intentions of the researcher for collecting and analyzing data of this kind. Here, the section referring to collaborative studies with the people in the study is very interesting for other forms of qualitative research, too. The same might be the case with the passage addressing the use of visual approaches as a way of seeing the world through the participants' (e.g. children's) eyes as a way of taking the perspective of the members in a field. Finally, the way this book addresses the tension between producing materials for research (in this case visual material) and taking already existing materials as data, can be very fruitful for research based on other sorts of data and materials. We also find considerations of planning research of this special type and about how to assess the quality of such a research in a specific way, which are complemented by the first and the last books in *The SAGE Qualitative Research Kit* (Flick, 2007a, 2007b) and at the same time complement them with some extra suggestions.

1
Introduction

Chapter objectives
After reading this chapter, you should

- see why the use and study of images in social research as one among various methodologies employed is justified;
- see the distinction between image creation and image study;
- understand the place of visual methodologies in the research process;
- know some key terms and concepts; and
- have an overview of the book.

Case study: Visual methods and hypothesis testing

For visual anthropologists, as well as many other visual studies scholars, Sol Worth and John Adair's 'Through Navajo eyes' project of the late 1960s is one of the landmarks in visual research. Although there have been criticisms of the project, it stands out as an example of well-designed empirical research, with clear objectives and methodologies. Worth (a communications scholar and anthropologist) and Adair (an anthropologist and linguist) set out to see if people who had little or no exposure to cinema and moving images would make films that reflected the way they saw the world in general. In particular, would the

(Continued)

(Continued)

FIGURE 1.1   Alta Kahn shooting *Navajo Weaver II*, Pine Springs,
Arizona, July 1966 (photograph by Richard Chalfen)

Navajo be able to 'bypass' language in communicating their world-view. The premise for the investigation rests on what is known as the Whorf–Sapir hypothesis – the idea that the structure of the language one speaks conditions how one sees and understands the world around one. Speakers of very different and unrelated languages, English and Navajo for example, will, in Whorf's words, 'cut nature up, organize it into concepts, and ascribe significances' in very different ways (Whorf, 1956, p. 214). While there have been various attempts to test the hypothesis, up to this point these mostly relied on language itself to conduct and assess the investigation in a rather circular fashion. Worth and Adair's breakthrough was to identify and use another channel of communication.

(Continued)

(Continued)

Worth, Adair and Worth's student Dick Chalfen gave 16 mm film cameras to seven Navajo people, living in a relatively traditional community in Arizona, where many older people spoke only Navajo, although the filmmakers were all bilingual. The seven had all seen some films but only one of them (an artist) had seen many. On the other hand, none of them was what Worth and Adair call 'professional Navajo' (1972, pp. 72–3), in the sense that they were self-consciously aware of Navajo traditions and customs and used to representing them to others. After they had been given basic instruction in shooting and editing, the Navajo were free to film whatever they wanted. Their final films consisted of short, silent, documentaries on topics such as silversmithing, weaving and Navajo curing ceremonies.

The results broadly confirm a 'weak' version of the hypothesis: 'language is a guide to social reality' (Sapir), not determinative of it. In assessing the way in which the Navajo filmmakers edited sequences of action, Worth and Adair noted on the one hand that the filmmakers did not discover and adopt the principle of continuity cutting common to Western film traditions (i.e. they saw 'jump cuts' as unproblematic), while on the other hand, certain sequences of apparently over-long or pointless action (such as a weaver winding up an entire skein of wool into a ball) could be linked to particular Navajo ideas about 'action' that are themselves linguistically distinctive in the Navajo language. Although the findings of the 'Navajo eyes' project are not wholly conclusive (some films, for example, could not be 'read' by some Navajo viewers, although tellingly one informant said she could not understand one film because it was 'in English'; in fact the films were all silent), it is nonetheless a pioneering early use of visual methods to address a particular research question. The original 1972 monograph describing the project was revised twenty-five years later by Dick Chalfen, who summarizes much of the subsequent debate (Worth and Adair, 1997).

Why (not) pictures?

Why should a social researcher[1] wish to incorporate the analysis of images – paintings, photographs, film, videotape, drawings, diagrams and a host of other images – into their research? There are two good reasons, though the first is easier to prove than the second, and there is also one caveat.

The first good reason is that images are ubiquitous in society, and because of this some consideration of visual representation can potentially be included in all studies of society. No matter how tightly or narrowly focused a research project is, at some level all social research says something about society in general, and given the ubiquity of images, their consideration must at some level form part of the analysis. Of course, the same could be said of music, or clothing, or many other aspects of human social experience. Yet while many valuable studies of these phenomena exist, none seems to have assumed the sensory prominence within social research that images have, sound (in the form of language) perhaps excepted. Some suggestions as to how this has come about are presented in the next chapter.

The second good reason why the social researcher might wish to incorporate the analysis of images is that a study of images or one that incorporates images in the creation or collection of data might be able to reveal some sociological insight that is not accessible by any other means. While this is self-evidently true of research projects that focus on visual media, such as a study of the effects of television viewing on children, it is less self-evidently true – and much harder to prove – in other projects. It is relatively easy to triumph the findings of some piece of visual research (some examples are given in later chapters), but less easy to prove that the same insights could not have been generated by an alternative research methodology. One would have to set up a series of research investigations into the same topic, with the same research subjects, each identical but for the research method employed, and each using researchers who were unaware of the findings of the other teams. While this might be possible in a laboratory context for a set of psychological experiments, say, the number of variables would spin out of control when attempted in a field setting. I return to this issue in the book's conclusion, but until then I confine myself to describing the distinctiveness of visual research processes and their findings rather than making claims as to their uniqueness.

The difficulty of setting up the experimental conditions to test one research methodology against another leads me to the caveat. Regardless of the existence of books and manuals such as this, devoted to a single social research methodology, in practice social researchers employ a number of different methodologies in their investigations, ranging from the highly formalized (certain types of image content analysis, closed interviewing schedules containing internal consistency checks) to the highly informal (chatting to people, observing daily activity). To restrict oneself to a single methodology or area of investigation is as sociologically limiting as wilfully ignoring a methodology or area. This book is an attempt to make the case that visual research methodologies are distinctive, are valuable, and should be considered by the social researcher whatever their project. It is not an attempt to claim that these methodologies supplant all others. Visual research should be seen as only one methodological technique among many to be employed by social researchers, more appropriate in some contexts, less so in others.

Being visual

Case study: Seeing through the eyes of children

Many sociologists and anthropologists have experimented with giving cameras (still or moving) to research subjects in order to 'see' the world as their research subjects see it. Although there are problems with this method, usually involving the interpretation of the resulting images, it can be particularly useful when conducting research with people who might find it difficult to express themselves verbally in the context of a formal interview – those with learning difficulties, for example, or children who might otherwise become bored.

Sharples et al. (2003) set out to explore not so much what children 'see' as how children understand photography in the first place. Disposable cameras were given to 180 children in five countries across Europe, drawn from three age groups (7, 11 and 15). The children were given a weekend to photograph whatever they liked and were then interviewed about their pictures. Some of the findings might have been expected; for example, the youngest children tended to photograph toys and other possessions, while the oldest children showed a preference for groups of friends. Equally, younger children enjoyed their photographs largely for their content alone, while older children had a growing appreciation of style and composition. But the researchers also conclude that the children's photographs are not merely their 'view of the world' but an indication of their perceived place in the world, particularly with regard to kinship and friendship relations. One finding was that children were generally 'scathing' of adult photography, and saw their parents' use of photography as indicative of their adult power.

In another study, Mizen (2005) gave 50 children cheap cameras and asked them to compile a 'photo-diary' of their work experience. This formed one element of an investigation into children's employment in England and Wales (between the ages of 13 and 16 children may legally be employed in what is known as 'light work', which does not affect their schooling or health). The cameras were introduced roughly halfway through a year-long period of qualitative research, during which the children had already been keeping written diaries, having interviews with research staff, and so on. One of the aims of the project, and one that particularly justified the use of cameras, was to find out 'what the children had to tell us about their work (rather) than the usual preoccupation of researchers with what the work has to tell us about the children' (Mizen, 2005, p. 125). Unsurprisingly, given that the children were themselves the photographers, there were few images of children actually working, and indeed very few pictures of people at all (including employers and co-workers). What the images did show was the character of the children's work, through documentation of their workplaces.

(Continued)

(Continued)

Mizen points out that there are no studies that have directly observed children at work in the 'affluent economies of the North' and so the photographs allow him and his co-researchers direct access to the structure, form and content of the work, but more particularly to the children's engagement with it. In particular, Mizen claims that although only around 5 per cent of the photographs showed employers, they were an invisible presence (in several instances they had asked the children to cease taking photographs) and relations with employers became a research theme that was subsequently developed with the children in interviews. Thus although both Sharples et al. and Mizen had quite different research agendas and employed quite different forms of subsequent analysis (Sharples et al. used two kinds of quite formalist analysis: see Chapter 3), the use of the same visual methodology produced rather similar findings concerning power relationships between children and adults.

What precisely are visual methodologies? While this question is addressed in detail in the rest of this book, particularly in Chapter 4, which considers methods in a fieldwork context, some basic points need to be established early on. Broadly speaking, there are two main strands to visual research in the social sciences. The first revolves around the creation of images by the social researcher (typically photographs, film and videotape, but also drawings and diagrams) to document or subsequently analyze aspects of social life and social interaction. In a field-based or even a laboratory context, the social researcher will undoubtedly be taking notes on the spot, perhaps muttering into a tape recorder, but she may also be taking photographs, making quick pencil sketches, and so forth. Back in the office, the social researcher may be turning lists of numbers into graphs, drawing up flow diagrams to show how one social event leads to another, analyzing sequences of videotape for repeated hand gestures, and so forth.

All these methods involve the creation of images by the social researcher, independently of whether the research subjects know about, understand, or even care about these images. The aim of such a project may not be specifically visual. For example, an investigation into the role of formal schooling in the creation and maintenance of gender stereotypes might involve the creation of many hours of videotape, numerous still photographs, and perhaps a number of visually based psychological tests, but few if any of these might be presented in the final research report or even referred to in detail. Even if the research was intended to be visual, or the findings revealed a visual outcome – for example, the hypothetical research above revealed that gender stereotypes are communicated visually as much as verbally in the classroom – then the researcher may still face constraints preventing her from publishing this. The power of the word is such that few journals would be prepared to print more than a few photographs, and no print-based ones would be able to present video. Similarly, it is rare that an image (as opposed to text about an image) is cited in the work of others, again leading to a disincentive to publish images. (Some possible solutions to this problem are presented in Chapter 5, in the section on presenting visual research.)

The second strand of visual research revolves around the collection and study of images produced or consumed by the subjects of the research. Here the focus of the research project is more obviously visual and the research subjects more obviously have a social and personal connection with the images. In the field, the researcher will be spending time with subjects watching television, or flicking through magazines, observing them as they videotape wedding ceremonies, or take photographs at children's birthday parties. Back in the office she will be transcribing interview notes about the television programmes watched, or studying copies of the photographs they took. These methods stem directly from the visual media themselves and from the research subjects' engagement with these media. Regardless of the difficulties, it is probably more necessary for the researcher to publish and disseminate her visual findings in this strand of research.

Briefly stated, these two strands can be contrasted as, on the one hand, the use of images to study society and, on the other, the sociological study of images. Methodologies for both sets are covered in Chapter 4, though the emphasis in that chapter is more on image creation in the study of society, while in Chapter 3 a number of analytical strategies towards the study of images of society are considered.

The two strands are not mutually exclusive, nor are they exhaustive of all visual research within the social sciences. In either approach, depending on the project, the social researcher will still be conducting surveys, interviewing subjects, collecting life histories, and so on. The former strand – the creation of images as an aid to studying society – is perhaps the older. Photography has been used to document and diagrams used to represent knowledge about society since the beginnings of modern sociology and anthropology in the nineteenth century. The latter strand – the sociological study of images – has grown in strength in the second half of the twentieth century, with the rise of film studies, media and communication studies, and a more sociologically informed art history. But in recent years a third strand has developed, one that encompasses the other two. This is the creation and study of the collaborative image and it is deployed in projects where social researcher and the subjects of study work together, both with pre-existing images and in the creation of new images. This development is informed by fundamental changes in social science epistemology, sometimes referred to as 'the postmodern turn'. The historical development of these strands and the corresponding theoretical insights that inform them are described in more detail in the next two chapters.

Planning and executing a visual research project

By the time they have reached the end of this book, together with the other volumes in this *Kit* (in particular Flick, 2007a; Gibbs, 2007; Kvale, 2007; and Rapley, 2007) and any other works on quantitative and qualitative research methodology thought relevant, social researchers should be able to construct an innovative and fully justifiable research project and be able to execute it on time and within budget through to the final dissemination of results. In broad outline, constructing a project involving visual methods is no different from preparing and executing any research proposal, though obviously the detail of any visual methods to be used will need to be given particular attention and justification.

Choosing a method

In general, it is not a good idea to begin planning a research project with a partic-ular method in mind and then casting about for an empirical subject to try it out on. Equally, it is not generally a good idea to begin with a subject and then think of a method or suite of methods to investigate it (though in practice, many research projects begin life this way). Ideally, one should formulate an intellectual problem, then consider the most suitable subject or empirical context for investigation, and then consider which methods within that context are most likely to yield data that will address the problem. I doubt all social researchers will agree with me on this line and in fact, in my experience, most independent social research begins with a concrete substantive issue (see also Flick, 2007a, 2007b).

For example, a researcher may be interested in why British teenage boys of Afro-Caribbean origin generally do less well than their white counterparts in for-mal education. She may have been led to this question by her own previous expe-rience, or through a newspaper report, or by some other means. An investigation that starts and finishes with this question and its answer is, to be honest, of lim-ited value, however well executed the research. Lying behind the question are one or several more general sociological problems of which this is only a concrete instance. One such sociological problem might be: is inequality within society structured and sedimented through social institutions or is it the cumulative effect of minor acts of social agency? With this question in mind, the study of differen-tials in boys' educational attainment now becomes broadened out, indeed to the point where visual methodologies could profitably be employed. For example, boys – and girls – could be given disposable cameras to photograph the places at home, in the street and at school where they feel most 'free'; or pupils could be asked to watch and then comment on a number of Hollywood action films that show hero-figures fighting back at society or against injustice, and so forth. I argue in Chapter 6 that image-based research often encourages investigative serendipity, the following of a line of inquiry that could not have been predicted in the original research design. Following such lines, however, can only be fruitful if the intellectual parameters are sufficiently broad to encompass them, hence the need for a general sociological problem lying behind the specific research problem.

Thus, the line from intellectual abstraction, to particular scenario, to appropriate method is worth defending. Even in contract and policy-related research, which is always driven by real-world problems (e.g. educational failure) rather than intellectual inquiry (e.g. the balance of structure and agency), it is important. For one thing, if the empirical conditions turn out not to be as expected, or the research cannot be executed as planned for some reason, then the underlying intellectual problem can be revisited to provide another empirical test case. More profoundly, without a point of origin in a body of theory and intellectual abstraction (even if located there after the event), the findings and output of any particular study are difficult to take further or generalize – indeed, their very significance may be opaque. While this may seem simply to be a defence of pure or 'blue skies' research and of intellectual integrity and independence, there are practical methodological consequences. For example, many so-called ethnographic films, produced as a mode of inquiry into the social life of another society, appear to have no intellectual underpinning from within, in this case, the discipline of social anthropology. Consequently, few social anthropologists who are not already film fans are prepared to give them much credence as a contribution to the discipline.

In some social science disciplines, establishing the intellectual underpinnings and then deciding upon the empirical context for investigation results in the creation of a hypothesis that can then be tested (for example, voter turnout at elections is correlated with the state of the economy, such that fewer people vote when the economy is strong; or, prolonged exposure to violence on television in childhood results in more persons becoming more violent in adulthood). In such cases, the choice of research methodologies is generally straightforward, relying on past practice and the tried-and-true. In other social science disciplines – including my own of social anthropology – there is a sense that the framework of hypothesis creation and testing forecloses the process of research too early and does not allow for unanticipated correlations or simple serendipity. Here, the programme of research is dictated by a more loosely formulated research question rather than a formal hypothesis (for example, why don't people bother to vote? or what is the role of social memory in the judgement of television programmes as 'violent'?), and the choice of method consequently becomes more open, responding to shifts in the direction of inquiry. In more critical mode the researcher might also go on to ask: in whose interest are these questions asked? Whose agenda does it serve to ask why people do not vote, or what constitutes 'violence' in the first place? In such research contexts, the choice of method consequently becomes more open and a variety of methods can be deployed in a spirit of disinterested inquiry.

In general, visual research methodologies tend towards the exploratory rather than the confirmatory. That is, visual methodologies are not so much employed as a method to gather data of predetermined size and shape that will confirm or refute a previously posited hypothesis, but as a method designed to take the researcher into realms that she may not have considered and towards findings previously unanticipated.

Some practical matters

With these discussions in mind, the construction of a research programme that employs visual methods can now proceed. Once a research question or hypothesis has been arrived at, its connection to a wider body of theory understood, and a specific empirical area of inquiry identified, questions of budget, timetable, research ethics and research methodology need to be addressed, and consideration given to dissemination and publication of the results. A variety of visual methods and forms of dissemination are discussed in later chapters, as are ethics, but some points concerning budget and timetable should be mentioned from the outset. Budgetary consideration should be given not just to the cost of consumables (film, videotape, batteries, digital camera data cards, and so on), but also to the – sometimes unexpected – costs associated with distribution (copies of photographs for return to research subjects, blank CDs, DVDs or videotapes, plus postage costs, for distributing film or video footage). Photographic reproduction costs in particular can be very high if the researcher plans or becomes involved in an exhibition of photographs as part of the research process (see the discussion of Geffroy's work in France in Chapter 5).

That such costs are not always anticipated is related to my opening comments on the ubiquity of images in society. I suspect that there are few people who have been the subject of an academic research project who would be delighted to receive a copy of a professional peer-reviewed academic paper, still less actively request a copy from the author. Conversely, most people who have been filmed, photographed or videotaped as part of a visual research project are very pleased to receive copies, and some do indeed actively demand them. Why should this be, given that the printed word is as ubiquitous as the visual image, at least in some societies? The answer is discussed more fully in Chapter 5, but relates to what some have called the polyvocality of images, their ability to permit multiple readings. To a researcher in behavioural studies, a photograph she took of two elderly men gesturing as they converse on a park bench is evidence of ethnic variation in non-linguistic communication and an important piece of evidence in her research report. To the niece of one of the men, it is treasured memory of recently deceased Uncle Luigi with his great pal Joe. The niece might well be interested to read that 'to reinforce his point, subject A (an elderly Italian-American male) gestures by bringing his right hand down in a closed fist upon the open palm of his left hand, while subject B (an Irish-American) looks on', but she is hardly likely to frame the page of the article and place it on her mantelpiece.

Research project timetabling is less likely to be subject to research subjects' demands, though the researcher with a video camera should be prepared to meet requests to record wedding ceremonies, children's birthday parties, and the like. What is likely is an underestimate of the time required to view, transcribe and analyze images produced or collected in the course of research. One immediate problem is that there is no cataloguing or classificatory scheme for either still or moving images in universal use, and there is currently very little that can usefully be achieved in the way of computerized image recognition.[2] This means that most researchers end up indexing their visual materials by hand and to a scheme of their own devising, which normally has to be revised several times along the way. A more detailed discussion of these procedures can be found in Chapter 5.

Key terms and concepts

Although a glossary is provided at the end of this book, visual research employs a large number of specialist terms, often terms in use in daily language but with a distinctive aspect that need to be examined more closely. As with much analytical language in the social sciences, many terms have a literal meaning elsewhere but are used metaphorically; it is always worth reminding oneself of the literal meaning from time to time nonetheless.

Agency

This term is commonly understood in the social sciences to mean the capacity of one person to act upon another, or to influence a set of social relations as a result of such action, and is normally invoked within discussions of power. The relationship between a person's agency, and the structures that constrain the totally free expression of that agency (structures such as a legal framework, the educational system, kinship relations, or 'tradition'), form one of the core areas of investigation within the modern social sciences. Although the term is normally confined to human agents, some anthropologists and others have attributed agency to objects: in the area of visual research, this is best summed up by Mitchell's provocative question, 'What do pictures really want?' (1996, cited in Edwards, 2001, p. 18). While some, especially in science and technology studies, appear to write and construct theory as though objects really were possessed of agency (see Latour, 1991, for an example), most tend to use the term more metaphorically or, following the anthropologist of art, Alfred Gell, in seeing the agency of persons displaced into objects ('secondary agency': see Gell, 1998). An

11

object, such as a photograph or a piece of art, makes us do things (such as bid a high price at an auction to acquire it) because that is the intention of its creator or owner, or others associated with it or, more sociologically, because a nexus of human social relationships imbues the object with apparently agentive action, regardless of the wishes of any particular individual. Leading on from the idea that images, whether in their own right or as tools of human others, have agency, it therefore follows that images do 'work'. The work that images do or do not do is relevant, for example, to the discussion of the use of photography in attempts to understand the Indian caste system, discussed in the next chapter (the section on early uses of photography).

Data

Although the term is normally associated with a more positivist version of social science than I am comfortable with, it is a convenient shorthand term. I use it throughout this book simply to indicate the objects of sociological attention. From a more positivist perspective the data are already 'out there' waiting to be discovered, while from a more intrerpretivist point of view the data are brought into being through the process of inquiry; either way, they are all data. In this book, the term simply denotes the visual images and other things that are identified, created or reified by the processes of social research into objects that can be manipulated, tabulated, compared one against another and so forth, regardless of their ontological status. Put another way, visual objects such as photographs can either be considered as data in their own right ('43 per cent of the images in the collection are glass-plate negatives'), or they can be considered as sources of data ('in 43 per cent of the images men are performing agricultural tasks'). For those of a less positivistic per-suasion, the latter meaning is more problematic because it relates to an interpretation of content (the internal *narrative*, see below), however apparently objective or obvious. The former understanding is easier to accept, referring as it does to the physical actuality of the object, the most basic aspect of its external narrative. (See also Box 2.1 in Chapter 2.)

Documentary

Although today the term is routinely applied to most if not all kinds of non-fiction film and some kinds of still photography, on the whole it is associated with the films of British filmmaker John Grierson and his mission, from the late 1920s onwards, to 'dramatize [social] issues and their implications in a meaningful way [which would] lead the citizen through the wilderness' of social change and uncertainty, as Erik Barnouw puts it (1983, p. 85). In other words, a documentary film – or corpus of documentary photographs – is not merely a neutral document or record of things that took place before the camera, but a *representation* (see below) of those things, persons and events intended to explain society and its processes to its citizens.

Figure/ground

In fine art or in descriptive assessments of images, the figure is the main subject of, say, a painting (for example, a vase of flowers or a bowl of fruit in a still-life) and the ground is more or less everything else (which in classical representational European art is normally the background – mountains, buildings, trees, etc., though not necessarily). Less literally, however, the terms are also used to explore the relationship between things that appear to be significant and those that seem incidental and also the extent to which figure is only given meaning by its relationship to ground (in gestalt psychology, for example). In the psychology of perception, a classic case is the simple black and white sketch, familiar to most children as an 'optical illusion', which can be seen either as the silhouette of two faces in profile facing one another as though in conversation, or as an elaborately shaped vase, depending on which of black or white is assigned the value of 'figure' and which 'ground'.

Frame

There are two literal uses one might encounter: (i) the physical, material frame in which a picture is placed when, for example, selecting a suitable frame to exhibit the photographs taken during a field investigation, or perhaps when considering the frame used to hold a family snapshot or memorial portrait that an informant is discussing in the course of an interview; (ii) when looking through the viewfinder of a camera to frame a shot, or when considering the frame that another photographer selected for a shot. These uses of the term concern relatively practical matters, although especially in the latter case this is not without theoretical or analytical importance. More commonly researchers encounter the term in a more metaphorical sense. Sociologists sometimes speak of the 'research frame', indicating what is, and is not, to be included in the investigation. For example, a piece of research into the correlation between children's educational attainments and family income would be unlikely to consider shoe size as a significant variable, and therefore not include it in the research frame. However, in contemporary Euro-America, children's choice of and access to certain brand-name (training) shoes might be significant and probably should be included within the research frame (Nike or Adidas?). In visual research the frame initially appears to be the frame around the image as published or experienced, but further investigation often shows that the frame needs to be considerably broadened. This can be taken in both a literal sense – what is *not* shown, just beyond the frame of the image seen? – as well as metaphorically – what social and hence sociological factors influence the photographic frame selected? Research investigations directed towards an image's external narrative (see below) often broaden the frame considerably.

Narrative

At its broadest, the term refers to the intentional organization of information apparently presented within – for our purposes – an image or sequence of images. More narrowly, and deriving from the use in academic as well as non-academic speech, it refers to the 'story' told by these images. At this point cultural speci- ficity must be highlighted: not all societies would necessarily recognize the logi- cal ordering of events that make a 'good' story for Euro-Americans. Narrative structures are established and understood by convention and are not innate or universal. In this book, however, as elsewhere (e.g. Banks, 2001), I take the broader meaning of the term, but distinguish two kinds of narrative – internal nar- rative and external narrative. The internal narrative of, say, a photograph is sim- ply addressed by the question: 'What is this a picture of?' (answer, in a descrip- tive mode: a cat, a woman, a man with a gun; but, more interpretatively, also: my pet, his wife, a murder). The external narrative is the story constructed by answer- ing such questions as: 'Who took this picture?', 'When was it taken?', 'Why was it taken?' Although some clues to aid in constructing the external narrative of an image can be derived from the image itself, for the most part the external narra- tive is constructed by conducting research elsewhere: in brief, by considering the image as a node or a channel in a network of human social relations. Such an exercise enlarges the (metaphorical) *frame* of the image (see above) to consider persons and events that may extend quite widely in time and space.

Ocularcentrism

This ungainly term refers to the apparent privileging of vision above all other senses in contemporary Western society (and increasingly elsewhere). The impor- tance of vision as a way of knowing the world is associated with the rise of modernity and subsequently postmodernity, partly because of the sheer volume of images that surround us in these periods (magazines, television, advertising hoardings, etc.) and partly because, as the French sociologist Michel Foucault has observed, vision becomes a tool and a means by which power is exercised in society. His most famous example, and one much cited and drawn upon since, is the panopticon, the eighteenth-century design for a prison in which the warders can see all the prisoners but cannot be seen by the prisoners (see Chapter 3). For some researchers ocularcentrism is merely a descriptive term, morally and socially neutral; for others it is implicitly a term of criticism, associated with the perpetual surveillance of modern life in the form of CCTV cameras on every street corner (see also Rose, 2001, p. 9). For the social researcher interested in visuality (the social construction and use of vision) it is ironic that the social sciences, like most other branches of academic study, are profoundly logocentric, preferring the word over the image to present their findings.

Perspective

This again is a term with both a technical meaning (as in 'vanishing-point perspective' as a compositional rule in fine-art painting and technical drawing) and everyday more casual and metaphorical usage, which is constantly invoked in social science, including visual research. One reason for including it here in this list is that its use normally implies a knowing – and seeing – agent, someone from whose perspective something is observed.

Reflexivity

Described more fully in Chapter 3, a reflexive approach in social research implies an awareness of the researcher's own role in the research process (as Becker, 1998, puts it, 'how to think about your research while you're doing it'). This can range from a minimal awareness of one's own biases or subjectivities to a full-blown autobiographical frame for the research. The mode of investigation, and the type of data considered, influence the level of reflexivity to some extent. For example, an analysis of public images used in advertising may require the researcher to confront her own subjectivity – as a woman, as a mother, as a consumer, and so on – but probably only to a minimal degree, or not at all. A project involving the creation and subsequent analysis of a community video, on the other hand, may involve a great deal of consideration of the researcher's relationship to the community in question, which itself will be predicated on her age, gender, class position, and so forth.

Representation

This term dominates much writing on the visual in both sociological writings and that of other disciplines, such as art history. The key point, in the case of visual representation, is that the thing seen – the representation – is a thing in its own right, not merely a substitute for the thing unseen, the thing represented. As Elizabeth Chaplin, amongst others, notes, a (visual) representation has three additional properties: its form is not dictated solely or even at all by the thing represented but by a set of conventions or codes (vanishing-point *perspective*, for example, allows a three-dimensional scene to be represented in two dimensions but only to viewers who understand the convention); it is embedded in, reflects and constitutes social processes (so, for example, a two-dimensional painting of a landscape may reflect and thus represent the wealth and aspirations of the landowner who commissioned it); and finally, the representation has some kind of intentional force behind it (see *agency* above) and presumes a viewer or a consumer

15

(for example, the viewer of the landscape painting) is impressed, even awed, by the landowner's wealth and ownership of such beauty (Chaplin, 1994, p. 1). But as Chaplin also notes, terms such as 'representation', 'picture', 'image' and so on are often used loosely in the literature, and readers are advised to study the context within which a term is used in order to assess the specificity of meaning intended (Chaplin, 1994, p. 183).

Organization of this book

This rest of this book is organized in the following way. Chapter 2 briefly outlines the history of visual methods in various social science disciplines and points to some key moments; initially popular in the late nineteenth century, the methodological use of still and moving images increasingly fell out of favour as researchers turned to what they considered to be more robust methodologies and as they discovered images to be far less pliant than they had imagined. It was only in the latter decades of the twentieth century that the expressive power of images began to be seen as a way of enriching sociological analysis. The point of the chapter is to indicate that there is little new in the current enthusiasm for visually oriented research and that an awareness of past ventures can provide a firm background.

Chapter 3 surveys a number of current analytical approaches towards the study of visual materials, while Chapter 4 outlines a number of recent field-based methods suitable for visual research. While in the course of an actual social research project, a researcher will normally collect (or generate) visual materials (or 'data') first, and go on to analyze them subsequently, I have a good reason for placing the analysis chapter before the methods chapter. Simply, most researchers today would recognize that there is no such thing as value-free data gathering. At the most basic or weakest level, human intentionality – the decision of a researcher to conduct a piece of research – presumes some kind of prior epistemological standpoint. More strongly, all researchers are likely to have some kind of theoretical or analytical intention in mind before executing the research. Consequently, it is necessary to examine those intentions before actually commencing the investigation, and consequently Chapter 3 precedes Chapter 4.

Chapter 4 falls into three main sections in which the visual field research methods described progressively become more active and engaged. After a brief introduction, the first section considers methods that largely utilize found, or preexisting, images, such as photo-elicitation. The following section then considers methodological issues that arise when social researchers create their own images, such as making ethnographic films. The final section moves on to consider a variety of collaborative strategies, in which the line between the researchers' interests and those of the people that she is researching is difficult to draw. The chapter concludes with a discussion of ethics in visual research. This section could perhaps have been placed at any point in the book and certainly ethical concerns permeate all aspects of the research process, from initial planning to the final report and beyond. But it makes sense to place it in the central chapter, to emphasize the centrality of the issue.

Chapter 5 moves from the field back to the academy and considers the ways in which visual research is presented. The 'audience' is an important consideration for a researcher, almost as important as the research itself, for if the research is poorly presented or targets the wrong audience, then much of the effort of research will have been wasted. The chapter considers two important audiences – fellow professionals, and the research subjects themselves – before going on to consider the value of computer-based systems that may help overcome some of the difficulties encountered in presenting visual research results.

The concluding chapter returns to some of the issues raised in the introduction with regard to the robustness of qualitative research methodologies, and particularly visual methodologies.

Images in the book

This book contains only a small number of images. I could have included far more – perhaps one for almost every sentence at some points in the text – and I also considered including none at all. To some extent the images introduce material that may be (visually) unfamiliar to many readers, and they are largely intended as illustrations, as a visual 'way in' to a point made in the text, rather than as 'data' to be analyzed. The relationship between image and text is discussed in Chapter 5, but after reading this book I hope the reader will bring a critical eye to all illustrated texts she encounters, both academic and non-academic. She should ask herself questions such as: why these pictures and not others? what work are these pictures doing – are they extending the text or supporting it? what lies beyond the frame? and, crucially, what sociological insights are these pictures providing?

Key points
- Visual research methodologies should only be used as part of a more general 'package' of research methodologies and their use should be indicated by the research itself, not just because the researcher enjoys taking pictures.
- Visual research can take longer than expected, and may involve additional costs; researchers should plan for this at the outset.
- In planning a project, researchers should try to identify the fundamental sociological questions that lie behind the specific investigation; at the same time, visual research methodologies are often used in an exploratory manner, to discover things the researcher had not initially considered.

Further reading

Skimming through a large number of short journal articles is a good way to get a feel for the field. Although there are no journals specifically devoted to visual methodologies in the social sciences, there are several devoted to visual analysis, and browsing through the articles published in these will give some insight into the range of methodologies possible. The main English-language journals are:

Visual Anthropology (Taylor and Francis, ISSN 0894-9468): located within sociocultural anthropology, publishes many articles based on fieldwork and archival research.

Visual Anthropology Review (University of California Press, ISSN 1035-7147): also located within sociocultural anthropology, but crossing over into cultural studies.

Visual Communication (Sage Publications, ISSN 1470-3572): no single disciplinary base but strong emphasis on semiotic analysis.

Visual Studies (formerly *Visual Sociology*) (Taylor and Francis, ISSN 1472-586X): grounded in sociology but including empirical fieldwork-based studies from a wide variety of disciplines.

2
The place of visual data in social research: a brief history

Chapter objectives
After reading this chapter, you should

- know about the history of image use in social science research, especially social anthropology and sociology;
- see the breadth and range of projects that have drawn upon image analysis; and
- understand that images are not neutral, transparent documents but constructed texts.

Case study: A.C. Haddon and the representation of the past

In anthropology and to a lesser extent in sociology there has always been an interest in the past, initially in the sense of reconstructing the past social forms of people studied, and more recently in understanding those people's own understandings of the past (see, for example, Davis 1989). In projects deploying visual research methods, however, the two may not always be so clearly distinguished.

(Continued)

(Continued)

In 1898 the British marine biologist-turned-anthropologist Alfred C. Haddon (see below, the section on early uses) led an ethnological expedition to the Torres Strait Islands, a group of islands between the northern tip of Australia and the island of New Guinea. His aim was to record the customs, language and other distinctive features of the islanders as they had been before European contact, some three decades earlier. The expedition was significant for many reasons, but one was in the extensive use of still photography and more limited use of a cine camera – itself a very recent invention.

FIGURE 2.1   (Torres Strait) A. C. Haddon (courtesy of Cambridge University Museum of Archaeology and Anthropology/Marcus Banks)

The sequence of frame stils above is taken from the first few seconds of the four or so minutes of film shot and shows three islanders performing a dance associated with an initiation cult. There are two important sociological issues to note: first, the cult itself had been abandoned when the islanders converted to Christianity; second, as a result of this, the original masks had been long since discarded and those worn in the film were made from cardboard packing material the night before filming. There is no evidence that Haddon coerced the islanders into making the masks or performing the dance (though he did pay them), and there is some evidence that the islanders, while remaining true to their Christian faith, saw the recreated dance as a way of re-engaging with their past and hence with their future. In some small way, Haddon's action facilitated a change in Torres Strait Islander social relations.

Thus, an apparently straightforward visual methodology – social performance and its capture by moving image recording technology as a way of bringing the past into the present for study – is at the same time a means by which people's engagement with the past, including the political ramifications of prior

(Continued)

(Continued)

social action (in this case, conversion to Christianity), can be brought to the fore. Although there is little evidence to suggest that Haddon had any sociological interest in this last point, recovery work of this kind has been done (see, for example, the essays in Herle and Rouse, 1998). More significantly, the example suggests that in any case where a social researcher asks a research subject to perform a piece of social action for the camera – and I intend 'perform' to be understood in the widest possible sense here – she or he at the same time opens up another line of inquiry and should ask how the research subject engages with their historic or other 'alternative' selves.

Introduction

Having considered the possible justifications for incorporating visual research methods into social research projects in the previous chapter, the next logical step might be to describe some of these methods. This is done in Chapter 4, but in this chapter and the next I wish to outline some background, key concepts and core analytical ideas. While the importance of getting the key concepts and core ideas clear should be self-evident, the need for a historical discussion may seem less so. There are a couple of reasons why I include a brief history here. First, the more we know about what has gone before, the better placed we are to devise or develop new methods that do not repeat what we can now acknowledge the mistakes of the past to have been. Equally there is a principle of economy to consider: why reinvent the wheel devising new methodologies or approaches, if all the hard work has already been done?

But there is another justification too. From the mildly reflexive analytical stance that I adopt in this book (see Chapter 3), it is an axiom that we as social researchers are as much sociologically – and intellectually – positioned as those we seek to investigate (see Becker, 1998). While some social science disciplines are relatively recent in development, and therefore have a relatively shallow history, my own discipline of social anthropology has at least a century and a half of history and development behind it. The motivating force of any anthropological investigation today, together with the methods used and the analysis applied, implicitly or explicitly reflects that history. In what follows I shall confine myself largely to key moments or developments of the use of visual materials in anthropology and sociology, with some brief nods towards psychology. As these are the oldest of the social science disciplines, it seems reasonable to presume that more recent disciplines, such as mass communication studies and cultural studies, draw upon them to some extent.

Box 2.1   Positivist and interpretivist approaches

Throughout this chapter and the rest of the book I make occasional reference to 'positivist' or 'interpretivist' approaches in social science. A positivist approach – sometimes and more accurately known as naturalist, and sometimes and inaccurately known as empiricist – is modelled on that of the natural sciences: data exist 'out there', independently of observation, and it is the researcher's job to gather them and study them, regardless of what the subjects who provided that 'data' thought about them, or indeed whether they even recognized them at all, as in the case of data generated by large-scale surveys and statistical analysis (see Hammersley and Atkinson, 1983, pp. 4–6). Interpretive approaches – also sometimes known as constructivist – which developed in the social sciences in the late 1960s, challenged the idea that human social action was subject to natural science-like laws that were sustained independently of that action.

Instead, it was argued that participants and social researchers alike interpreted social action according to a broader set of contexts and meanings. Social action such as ritual behaviour should be seen, as the American anthropologist Clifford Geertz famously put it, as a story that society tells itself about itself (Geertz, 1973, p. 448). Precisely because this 'story' is acted, not merely understood or held as a mental representation, meant that investigators had to consider the full 'performance' of social action – oral, visual, gestural – including the feelings and emotions of those involved.

With a positivist approach to social research it seems obvious that images, or at least photomechanical images such as film and photography, have little part to play. One cannot, for example, take a photograph of 'class', or 'kinship', or 'the economy', or any other such abstraction, though a photograph of a couple in their finery denotes a wedding (or more particularly Paul and Mary or whoever at their wedding) and also connotes whatever meaning 'weddings' have to the viewer (see Barthes, 1964, for the difference between denotation and connotation). Although some researchers vehemently advocate one approach or the other (for example, 'if we are to believe the many, many textbooks on social science method, positivism is alive and well in social science. It isn't, it's dead', Williams: 2002, p. 12), it is sensible to treat extreme claims with caution. This book advocates a largely interpretivist approach, but recognizes the value of some quantitative procedures that often depend upon a naturalist stance towards data collection, for example some forms of content and semiotic analysis (see Chapter 3).

Early uses of photography in social research

Sociology and anthropology developed (in their professional form) and grew to maturity with the rise of photomechanical image production techniques – first still photography and then cinematography. Still photography, with its apparent verisimilitude, was quickly allied to a number of sociological and governmental projects designed to objectify and sometimes quantify differences between individual persons and between groups of persons. Within anthropology we have the rise of anthropometric photography in the nineteenth century; in psychology at roughly the same time – at least in the popular realm – we have early experiments to capture states of mind; within sociology, the disciplinary use of photography is not seen until the middle of the twentieth century, but the use of photography to investigate and document social welfare dates back to at least the 1930s.

Early visual anthropology

Anthropometric photography was a project closely allied with Victorian anthropological ideas concerning the correlation of social and biological evolution. It was clear to Victorian anthropologists that the different societies with which they were familiar, both within Europe and outside it, differed one from another in their forms of social organization, their array of material culture, and so forth. It was also clear that members of some societies differed from members of other societies morphologically, in terms of their height, skin colour, bodily proportions, and so on. Drawing on pre-Darwinian ideas of biological evolution, some early anthropologists sought to typologize human societies on an evolutionary scale, arguing that some societies were closer to an original, or 'primitive', form of social organization than others. With the rapid spread of photography the idea grew that it might be possible to correlate these social differences at the level of individual morphological difference.[3] The most notable exponent of this method was Thomas Henry Huxley, a biologist, who in the 1860s devised a method to photograph colonial subjects in such a way that images of subjects from around the British Empire could be compared morphologically. The individuals, one each of a man, a woman and a child, were to be photographed unclothed, full face and in profile, standing next to a measuring scale (Edwards, 2001, pp. 137–8). If completed satisfactorily, one would be able to see – and therefore in a Foucauldian sense 'know' – the differences between what were often referred to as the 'races' of mankind.

Case study: Seeing social difference in colonial India

Right from their first encounters with Indian society, European observers observed a form of social division that appeared to have no counterpart with anything found elsewhere: 'caste' (from the Spanish and Portuguese *casta*, something not mixed). The closest observers could come to describing this phenomenon initially was by comparing the castes to 'races'(a common and

(Continued)

(Continued)

FIGURE 2.2 Undated postcard captioned 'Types of Indian women. The Kashmiri girls' (photographer unknown)

rather vague term in the seventeenth and eighteenth centuries, lacking the specific and grossly inaccurate biological associations of the late nineteenth and twentieth centuries), on the grounds that their forms of social organization seemed to differ and that marriage was not generally permitted between them. Written descriptions of these 'races' were produced from the eighteenth century onwards, but increasingly these were often accompanied first by drawings (of 'natives' in typical dress, for example) and then by photographs. Through photography of caste 'types' it was hoped that visual attributes of bodily morphology, dress and associated artefacts would reveal inner sociological truths. Photography was often employed in academic and administrative endeavours to judge human social difference, and nowhere more so than in India, where photographs of 'types' ranged side by side would help the

(Continued)

(Continued)

visitor and scholar to distinguish between different types of Indians (Pinney, 1997, pp. 28–9; see also Pinney, 1992).

But as more and more was learned about India and its peoples, so the picture (literally and metaphorically) became more, not less, confused. In particular, by the late nineteenth century there were at least two competing European views of Indian caste. One held that the castes differed one from another on the basis of the occupation that a caste's members actually or traditionally followed, while the other held that they were 'racial' groups, separated by blood and descent, whose occupational calling was incidental. As Christopher Pinney notes, quasi-anthropometric photography (that is, not necessarily conforming to Huxley's strict requirements) was deployed in support of both arguments, and in one case – tellingly – the same photographer's images were used in publications that Pinney claims supported both, opposed, assessments (Pinney, 1992, p. 168).

At much the same time as colonial officials and ethnologists were exploring the use of photography as a tool to document and make sense of other societies, professionals and amateurs in Europe and America were turning the camera on their own society. Two related projects in particular lie at the root of contemporary psychology and criminology. In the late nineteenth century, the Italian physician and criminologist Cesare Lombroso advocated a theory of criminal physiognomy by comparing dozens of photographs of arrested criminals and then seeking to determine if certain facial features were associated with certain types of criminal activity (Lombroso, 1887; see also Gould, 1981).

This was only one of a number of such projects whereby the camera was used to gain additional understandings into the 'bad', the criminal. The French criminal investigator Alphonse Bertillon had in the 1880s devised what is now the ubiquitous system of photographing criminals full face and in profile, though in this case the interest was more pragmatic, intended to help the Paris police force identify re-offenders. At the same time a similar photographic interest was being shown in the 'mad', the insane. Starting with Charles Darwin's ethological investigation into emotion (1872), which was illustrated with photographs of people showing fear, astonishment, and so forth, a variety of investigators sought, in a way similar to Lombroso, to pin down the 'look' of madness (see Rose, 1990, cited in Barry, 1995, p. 52). Darwin's work has been said to be methodologically pioneering in the study of emotion and facial expression (Poignant, 1992, p. 56), although subsequent assessments of such projects, especially those involving the criminal and the insane and drawing upon Foucault for inspiration, are often negative (but see Barry, 1995, p. 51). Peter Hamilton and Roger Hargreaves, however, point out that these photographic practices must be seen in context: at the same time as the camera was capturing and, in a sense, creating the mad and the bad ('the damned'), for example, it was also capturing and creating celebrity ('the beautiful') (Hamilton and Hargreaves, 2001).

Visual sociology and the Farm Security Administration

As noted above, the systematic use of still (or moving) photography was not part of the project of sociology until well into the twentieth century; Douglas Harper, for example, argues that 'visual sociology' as a subdiscipline did not come into being until the 1960s (though in the nominal sense the same could be said of visual anthropology) and the pioneering studies he cites from the 1960s and 1970s were inspired by the work of documentary photographers rather than sociologists (Harper, 1998, p. 28). Harper argues elsewhere that the (presumably innocent) failure of the Chicago School of sociology in the 1920s to use photography in their field-based investigations set the tone for what was to follow; the subsequent rise of survey- and interview-based research did nothing to counter this absence of visual methods (Harper, 1989, cited in Prosser, 1998, p. 103). The comparison with anthropology is telling. Although the anthropometric projects described above fell out of favour relatively quickly, as did eventually the social evolutionary theories that in part justified them, anthropology as a discipline had begun with images and continued to produce and consume them as 'illustrations', even during the arid decades of the 1930s to the 1960s when the discipline was dominated by intellectual concerns – and consequently methodologies – for which visual data were not thought necessary. Some of the journalistic visual precursors that Harper cites for post-Second World War visual sociology, however, are essentially sociological in intent, and some used well-systematized methodologies. Most notable is the work of photographers employed by the US Farm Security Administration (FSA) in the 1930s.

The FSA was set up in the wake of the Great Depression and the transformation of much of the American Midwest farmland into a dustbowl. As part of its strategy to gather as much information as possible about the situation of farmers and to do what it could to promote confidence at a time of economic and social uncertainty, the FSA commissioned teams of photographers to document farm and small-town life. The project was not sociologically uninformed; as Charles Suchar notes, the sociologist Robert Lynd (co-author of a classic work on the effects of the Depression [Lynd and Lynd, 1937]) helped devise the 'shooting scripts' employed by the FSA photographers (Suchar, 1997, p. 36). These 'shooting scripts' were not merely lists of subjects the photographers should attempt to capture ('production of foods . . . picking, hauling, sorting, preparing . . . field operations – planting; cultivation; spraying', etc.) but also statements of intended outcome ('People – *we must have at once*: Pictures of men, women and children

FIGURE 2.3   Boys looking at penny movies, 1938, Donaldson, Louisiana
(photograph by Russell Lee, coursty of the Library of
Congress)

who appear as if they really believed in the U.S. . . . . Too many [photographs] in
our file now paint the U.S. as an old people's home and that just about everyone
is too old to work or too malnourished to care what happens'). Lynd's particular
suggestions, however, went beyond such naïve listings and crude propaganda.
For example, after a list of suggested places where 'people' might meet, he adds,
'Do women have as many meeting places as men? It is probable that the women
in the lower-income levels have far less opportunity of mingling with other
women than women of the higher-income groups' – in other words, a sociological hypothesis that could be tested photographically.[4]

Early uses of film in social research

Any claim that anthropology was the major consumer and producer of still photography in the late nineteenth and early twentieth centuries probably needs further
research for verification. It is I think unquestionable, however, that the discipline
was – and continues to be – the major consumer and producer of film in the social
sciences. Although there are some claims to precursor status (see examples from
1894 onwards listed in Jordan, 1992), the first anthropological film fragment, a
four-minute sequence, was shot by the marine biologist-turned-anthropologist
A.C. Haddon in 1898 in the Torres Strait Islands, off the northern tip of Australia
(see case study at the start of this chapter), only three years after the first portable
moving picture camera had been developed.

By 1901, the anthropologist Baldwin Spencer was filming Aboriginal dances in Australia, and over the next two decades or so a number of anthropological expeditions were equipped with a film camera for documenting the customs and habits of the natives under investigation. By this time, the linkage between social evolutionary theory and still photography had largely been abandoned, and the impetus for anthropological film production and hence its use as a field methodology was documentary and, perhaps, pedagogic. It also continued a practice established with still photography for allowing images of remote persons and places to circulate amongst scholars who would never visit these locations themselves (Edwards discusses this process for still photographs in Chapter 2 of her *Raw Histories,* 2001). Many films from this period were made by or in association with, or were distributed to, ethnographic museums and concern aspects of material culture, and although this tradition died out in the UK by the 1930s (rather later in the US), it continued to be a dominant mode in European ethnographic film tradition, especially in German-speaking countries and Eastern Europe until comparatively recently.

In Western Europe and America a new direction came about in 1922 when the American explorer and filmmaker Robert Flaherty publicly released his influential *Nanook of the North.* While *Nanook* can be said in some respects to 'document' aspects of the lives of the Eskimo people (as they were then known) of Hudson Bay, Canada, it does so in a way that is driven by narrative, suspense, tension and resolution – qualities of the cinema or of theatre, not of anthropology or science.

More so than with still photography (at least until recently), the production and use of film in anthropology has always vacillated between two poles, that of the documentary and that of the cinematographic. This can in large part be attributed to the importance of cinema as a form of entertainment: the sheer mass and ubiquity of commercial feature film from the 1920s onwards meant that it is difficult to see how any anthropologist or other social researcher picking up a film camera in the decades since could not, at least subconsciously, have been influenced by it. Haddon's short sequences, shot before cinematographic conventions were established, look more like still photographs than anything else (recently a colleague, on seeing them for the first time, compared them to the animated magical photographs of J.K. Rowling's Harry Potter novels).

Yet by the time we get to lengthy and highly 'scientific' research films, such as the Oxford anthropologist Beatrice Blackwood's *Kukukuku* or *A Stone Age People in New Guinea* (1936–37) (concerned mostly with material culture), we are not viewing a neutral 'document' but a contrived and constructed piece of work, one that is conscious of camera angle, framing, and so forth. Yet *Kukukuku* seems innocent of this; it is shot in a naturalistic style and is barely edited. Blackwood was, I am in no doubt, seeking to make an accurate portrayal of stone axe production or whatever, covering all the aspects of the process in what seemed the most obvious way possible. Flaherty, by contrast, rather than choosing to ignore or suppress the dramatic potential of film, chose instead to work with it – to make use of what had so far been established by way of cinematographic convention to strengthen *Nanook* and his later films.

Professional anthropologists were pioneers in the use of film in the late nineteenth and early twentieth centuries. Yet the practical difficulties of film production, especially in hot, humid and physically inaccessible regions, combined with a lack (in Britain and America at least) of a strong intellectual justification for its use as a field methodology, meant that the bulk of 'ethnographic' film in the period before the Second World War (and, indeed, afterwards) was produced by enthusiastic amateurs rather than anthropologists. The one major exception is Margaret Mead and Gregory Bateson's work in Bali in the 1930s. Mead did have an intellectual basis for her approach, the so-called culture and personality school of American anthropology, deriving from the work of the linguist and anthropologist Edward Sapir, and strongly influenced by gestalt psychology. The basic idea was that the elements of 'culture' were organized into a whole that could be compared to a 'personality', and that through studies of child socialization in particular one could see the transmission and acquisition of this cultural personality.

Having already used this approach in her work on Samoa and New Guinea societies, deploying the conventional anthropological methodology of participant-observation, Mead decided to extend her methodology through the use of film and still photography. In all, she and Bateson took more than 25,000 still photographs (around 750 of which were selected for their main publication: Bateson and Mead, 1942) and 22,000 feet of 16mm film footage (approximately 15 hours' worth). Images, they felt, would be able to convey what words were inadequate to do: 'the intangible relationships among different types of culturally standardized behaviour' (1942, p. xii). Whether or not the project was a success is something I shall assess in the following chapter, but Mead and Bateson's work is referenced in even the briefest accounts of the history of visual anthropology (e.g. Morphy and Banks, 1997, pp. 10–11) or visual sociology (e.g. Harper, 1998, pp. 25–6) and has acquired near-iconic status.

Later uses of photography and film in social research

In Chapter 4, I survey a wide variety of contemporary uses of visual methods in social research. The purpose of this section is simply to briefly assess significant post-Second World War developments. Chief amongst these is a theoretical shift, in at least some parts of some social sciences, away from positivism and towards interpretivism. The second major development, again from the late 1960s, is the development of video as a cheap and convenient medium, although it was not really until the 1980s that cameras were small, light and cheap enough to be used by researchers. By the 1990s no social researcher that I know of was using 16 mm film, although the medium still remains popular among some professional documentary filmmakers.

Broadly speaking, until the late 1960s, the situation described in the previous section prevailed: anthropologists continued to use still photography in their work, but largely for illustrative purposes in lectures and publications, continuing the practice of presenting images of those under study to those who would never visit them, and helping to render those studied more familiar or human; in sociology, following the lead set by social documentary photographers, a few sociologists began to use the still camera to document social issues such as drug use and poverty (Harper, 1998, p. 28 cites a number of studies). In the world of film, however, the 1960s saw the rise of a generation of practitioners who had some anthropological training or who worked closely with anthropologists but were also professional filmmakers. While a very few anthropologists continued to use film by themselves, many more began to work with filmmakers to collaborate on projects. In some of these projects the aims of scientific documentation and creative cinematographic practice were in tension, with neither side really appreciating the aims of the other. The tension was particularly magnified when films were being made by or for television companies, which added the competing strain of commercial expectations.

In other projects, however, the collaboration drew upon the strengths of both impulses to great effect. Richard Hawkins's film *Imbalu: Ritual of Gisu Manhood* (1989), on ritual male circumcision amongst a group in Uganda, is an especially good example here. Combining the empirical research of anthropologist Susette Heald with the filmmaking expertise of Hawkins (as director) and David MacDougall (as camera operator), the film uses a compelling narrative device (the voiceover narration of one of the participants) and strong, engaged and engrossing camerawork to convey detailed analytical insight.[5]

The work that MacDougall and others went on to create in the 1970s and beyond also showed the ability of film (and still photography, though to a lesser extent until recently) to explore areas of social investigation that anthropology and sociology had ignored until then, but which were rapidly coming to prominence. With the arrival of interpretivist approaches the power of film and photography to particularize, but also to express, came to the fore. No amount of data on the frequency of women's fertility ceremonies in Maasai society (Kenya), or the ages of the participants, or the number of head of cattle owned by Maasi men, can get to the core of Maasai gender relations in the way that Melissa Llewelyn-Davies's film *The Woman's Olamal* (1984) does.

With the rise of interpretivist and phenomenological approaches in the social sciences, there has also been a shift away from language and linguistically derived models of society and towards studies oriented towards the body, to music and dance, and to feeling, emotion and memory. Written descriptions, and interview and survey methods, can go some way towards both recording and presenting such research, but film and photography not only enrich such studies, they can provide insight beyond that which is possible with mere words alone. Of course, such uses of investigator-generated visual representations are not exclusively interpretivist. Ethnomethodologists, for example, however phenomenological their mode of analysis, have generated and used visual data in an essentially positivist way, for example, in the use of static video cameras to gather 'data' that can augment conversational analysis (see Heath and Hindmarsh, 2002) – and areas of research such as proxemics and choreometrics (both concerned with the movement and placing of the human body in space) that developed from the 1960s were not especially interpretivist in either the creation of visual images or their analysis (see Lomax 1975; Prost 1975). Post-1960s developments in psychology and psychotherapy have also increasingly used photography in a way that lies somewhere between naturalism and interpretation (Cronin, 1998).

The rise of video since the 1960s, and especially the establishment of cheap, light and easy-to-use digital video cameras from the late 1990s, has seen an explosion in visual production by social scientists of all hues. As a result, there have been calls for some earlier working practices to be rethought. First, data-hungry disciplines such as ethnomethodology, proxemics and choreometrics have been freed from the constraints that cumbersome and expensive ten-minute reels of 16mm film imposed. In conversation analysis, for example, the earlier use of sound-recorded telephone conversations to provide data on informal linguistic interaction can now be enriched by studying video recordings for non-verbal cues (see Goodwin, 2001, for examples). Secondly, the status of ethnographic film as an enterprise that 'we' do to 'them' has been challenged as those filmed increasingly have access to video technologies themselves (e.g. Ginsburg, 1994). Finally, and staying with ethnographic film, some have argued that the time has come for anthropologists and others who collaborated with professional filmmakers in the past to break off the relationship and to retake control of the camera (e.g. Ruby, 2000, p. 239). I return to all these issues in the next chapter. There are of course many other theoretical and methodological shifts that have taken place since the 1960s, but the above passage is merely intended to outline some broad principles; specific examples are dealt with in subsequent chapters.

Other kinds of image use

So far, I have confined the discussion largely to the creation, and subsequent study, of photomechanically and photoelectronically produced images – still photographs, film and videotape – by the social researcher. Yet a great deal of social research has involved the use, and sometimes the creation, of other kinds of image. For various reasons discussed in Chapter 3, the analysis of pre-existing images does not form a major part of the discussion of this book, with certain exceptions. Similarly – again with some exceptions – the creation of images other than photographs, film and videotape is excluded.[6] Of course, social researchers have used and created visual representations from the start of the formal sociological project: tables, diagrams, graphs, bar charts, and so on. These are all forms of representation that generally have a reductive quality. Subtleties and fine texture are eliminated or smoothed out, 'data' are aggregated. This is often very useful, allowing the researcher to spot patterns and trends of sociological significance. At the same time, care must be exercised because if the wrong elements are eliminated or the wrong criterion for clustering adopted, then however tidy the final visual representation (a bar chart, a pie diagram), it can hide more than it can reveal.

I end this chapter with a particularly fine example of this, taken from the work of Edward Tufte. In his *Visual Explanations* (1997, one of three beautifully produced volumes devoted to the visualization of statistical and other quantifiable data), Tufte retells the famous story of Dr John Snow and the London cholera outbreak of 1854. During the month of September 1854 over 600 people died from cholera, the vast majority of them within a small area of central London; it was the worst outbreak of modern times. Snow, a physician who had investigated earlier cholera outbreaks, was on the scene quickly and attempted to derive a theory of disease transmission by examining information about the deaths. For the history of medical science, this was Snow's great breakthrough: he did not subscribe to the then popular idea that cholera was transmitted, even caused, by foul air or vapours, but suspected that the infectious agent was water-borne. From Tufte's point of view, Snow's great breakthrough was to use visual methods to pinpoint the exact water source responsible.

As Tufte shows, there are ways of presenting the mortality data visually that are apparently revealing but are in fact merely descriptive, not explanatory. For example, calculating the deaths by day, and cumulative deaths over the month, shows the speed and aggressiveness of the outbreak. Visually, bar charts showing these data most certainly say something about the rate of cholera transmission, but nothing at all about cause. Instead, Snow's brilliance was to combine iconic and symbolic visual representations (graphs are symbolic alone), by placing symbols representing deaths (at any time) onto a map of the local area. On this map (reproduced in Tufte, 1997, pp. 30–1), small bars representing deaths are placed against particular addresses on the streets. It is visually evident that the highest concentration of deaths occurred in and around Broad Street (present-day Broadwick Street, in Soho). Combined with the hypothesis that the infectious agent was water-borne (verified by the discovery and isolation of the bacterium some 30 years later), the mapped evidence seemed to indicate the water pump in Broad Street as the source. Confirmatory evidence also came from that which was not seen: for example, the densely crowded and almost certainly unsanitary workhouse north of the pump in Poland Street had far fewer cases than might be expected, only five, for the simple reason that it had its own independent water supply. There is obviously far more to be said about Snow's work and the importance of visual combined with other methods, but the case is clean and neat as it stands: the visual representation of quantifiable data yields a result that supports a hypothesis that can then be further tested.

Tufte, however, also cites the work of a mathematician, Mark Monmonier, author of the intriguingly titled *How to Lie with Maps* (1991). Taking the same data Snow had available to him, Monmonier redraws the map of the Soho area, aggregating the deaths in clusters by neighbourhood. Depending on the criteria selected to assign neighbourhood boundaries, the death clusters aggregate differently, to the point where they have no obvious visual association with the Broad Street pump at all! In this case, the visual method can conceal what it is supposed to reveal. The opposite scenario is perhaps more common: visual methods can reveal what was supposed to be concealed, or that which had been unanticipated.

In the next chapter I consider a range of analytical perspectives that can be taken towards visual materials, ranging from the formal (such as Tufte and Monmonier's interpretations of Snow's work) to the much more imaginative.

▭ Key points

- Visual methods have been used in social anthropological and socio-logical research for many decades; researchers should try to see as many previous examples as possible – films, photographic essays, and the like – to familiarize themselves with the range of possibilities.
- The meaning of images changes over time as they are viewed by different audiences; similarly, the meaning intended by the social researcher when she creates an image may not be the meaning that is 'read' by the viewer.
- Photographs and film or video are used rather differently by researchers who adopt either an interpretivist approach or a naturalist approach to the study of society; researchers should be clear about their own theoretical orientation before picking up a camera.

Further reading

De Brigard and Becker give overview accounts of the role played by images and image-making in the history of social science research; Griffiths, and the contributors to Edwards's and to Schwartz and Ryan's volumes, present modern analyses of historical images that were not necessarily intended as

(Continued)

(Continued)

sociological but can now be read for that purpose. Meanwhile, Pinney and Peterson (2003) provide an important cross-cultural perspective on photographic history.

Becker, H.S. (1974) 'Photography and sociology', *Studies in the Anthropology of Visual Communication*, 1: 3–26 [republished in H.S. Becker (1986) *Doing Things Together: Selected Papers*, Evanston: Northwestern University Press; also available online at lucy.ukc.ac.uk/becker.html.]

de Brigard, E. (1995 [1975]) 'The history of ethnographic film', in P. Hockings (ed.), *Principles of Visual Anthropology* (2nd ed.). The Hague: Mouton, pp. 13–43.

Edwards, E. (ed.) (1992) *Anthropology and Photography 1860–1920*. New Haven: Yale University Press in association with The Royal Anthropological Institute, London.

Griffiths, A. (2002) *Wondrous Difference: Cinema, Anthropology and Turn-of-the-Century Visual Culture*. New York: Columbia University Press.

Pinney, C. and Peterson, N. (eds) (2003) *Photography's Other Histories*. Durham, NC: Duke University Press.

Schwartz, J.M. and Ryan, J.R. (eds) (2003) *Picturing Place: Photography and the Geographical Imagination*. London: I.B. Tauris.

3
Approaches to studying the visual

Chapter objectives
After reading this chapter, you should

- know the principal forms of 'desk-based' visual analysis;
- be aware that even if no form of analytical perspective is consciously selected prior to research, researchers should nonetheless consider their own standpoint; and
- understand that visual forms are always material forms and that this must not be overlooked in analysis.

Case study: **Foucault on Bentham's panopticon**

Bentham's Panopticon is ... an annular building; at the centre, a tower; this tower is pierced with wide windows that open onto the inner side of the ring; the peripheric building is divided into cells, each of which extends the whole width of the building; they have two windows, one on the inside, corresponding to the windows of the tower; the other, on the outside, allows the light to cross the cell from one end to the other. All that is needed, then, is to place a supervisor in a central tower and to shut up in each cell a madman, a patient, a condemned man, a worker or a schoolboy. By the effect of backlighting, one can observe from the tower, standing out precisely against the light, the small

(Continued)

(Continued)

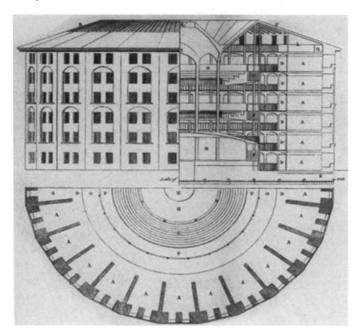

FIGURE 3.1   Bentham's panopticon
(Source: http://commons.wikimedia.org/wiki/Image:panopticon.jpg)

captive shadows in the cells of the periphery. ... The panoptic mechanism arranges spatial unities that make it possible to see constantly and to recognize immediately. In short, it reverses the principle of the dungeon; or rather of its three functions – to enclose, to deprive of light and to hide – it preserves only the first and eliminates the other two. Full lighting and the eye of a supervisor capture better than darkness, which ultimately protected. Visibility is a trap. (Foucault, 1977, p. 200)

Foucault uses this description of Bentham's 1787 plan for a panoptic penal institution as a metaphor for the power the modern state has over its citizens: a form of power through which the citizens regulate their own behaviour on the assumption that they are being watched, whether they can perceive this or not. Foucault's use of the panopticon model has been hugely influential in some branches of visual analysis, particularly in cultural studies perspectives in the 1980s and 1990s (see below). Here, the modern equivalent of the panopticon is often identified as the ubiquitous CCTV camera network of Euro-American cities (see, for example, Wood, 2003). It is estimated that the average London-dweller of the early twenty-first century passes before 300 CCTV cameras during the course of a working weekday (BBC News, 7 February 2002).

Introduction: theory and analysis

The history of visual methodology and visual analysis presented in the previous chapter was largely free from explicit discussions of 'theory', yet clearly such investigations did not take place in a theoretical vacuum. By 'theory' I do not simply mean grand theory (the theory of evolution, functionalist theory) but rather the theoretical presumptions that all social researchers, and indeed all of us (in the form of 'folk theory'), bring to our understanding of the world. In contemporary social thought it is now accepted that there is a dialectical relationship between what Richard Jenkins refers to as 'epistemological reflection and empirical research', and the relationship itself is the subject of critical reflection (Jenkins, 1992, p. 61–2).[7] The implication of this is that it is not possible to collect (visual) data in a purely mechanical fashion and then to sit down afterwards to decide what mode of analysis will be applied and what theoretical assumptions underlie that analysis. On the other hand, it would seem too constraining to work up the theory and analytical strategies first, and then embark upon targeted data gathering to meet the objective.

In order to understand the value and use of visual images in the production of sociological knowledge, it is therefore necessary to consider how different analytical stances approach what I have so far called 'data'.[8] In general, formal or realist (generally glossed as 'positivist') modes of analysis understand data items as ontologically distinct – something 'out there' that can be gathered and studied, much like botanical specimens. Interpretive analysis by contrast sees the things that are studied (the term 'data' is rarely used) as ontologically constituted through the act of study (see Box 2.1 in Chapter 2).

Another way of considering the field of analytical traditions is to make a distinction between those forms or styles of visual analysis that deal with the analysis of pre-existing images, and those that create the images and then subsequently analyze (or at least present) them. The latter is more commonly associated with empirical, and often fieldworking practices of social research, anthropology most obviously but also some traditions within sociology, development studies, psychology, social geography and educational studies; these empirical approaches are the subject of Chapter 4. The former mode – the analysis of pre-existing images – is generally practiced by scholars in the fields of communication studies, cultural and media studies, and information design, although sociologists, anthropologists and others have also contributed.[9]

As the emphasis of other books in *The SAGE Qualitative Research Kit* (e.g. Angrosino, 2007; Barbour, 2007; Kvale, 2007; Rapley, 2007) is largely upon the generation of data (through interviews, focus groups, and the like), the emphasis of this book lies more towards the study of images in the course of empirical field research. Such images may be generated by the social researcher (typically still photographs or videotape today), or uncovered by them in the archive or during the course of fieldwork, thus combining both approaches. My emphasis, however, is on the analysis of images in their social context (but see also Gibbs, 2007), a context that includes their production as well as their consumption (the full external narrative). At best, knowledge of the context of production is actively elicited through empirical investigation rather than merely presumed: for example, a study of advertising images, or urban graffiti, would seem to me to be sociologically incomplete if the author failed to interview any advertising executives about their choice of images, or any young people about their choice of locations for practicing graffiti art. Similarly, at the consumption end of things, a great deal of academic writing about film and fine art confidently assigns 'meaning' to images based, presumably, on the author's own reading, without apparently asking the intended viewers what they thought the images 'meant'.

Ways of seeing and things seen

As indicated in Chapter 1, it is difficult to imagine a social research investigation that does not – or that could not – employ images at some stage of the analysis. There are, however, numerous variations of the relationship between images and analysis. For example, in quantitative research, images such as tables, bar charts, graphs, etc., tend to arise out of and are another way of displaying the essentially textual or numerical data findings, while in more qualitative research the images are usually the subject of research and some kind of analysis will be performed on them.

Yet underlying these differences there are three basic points to consider. The first concerns the analytical approach taken towards the image, the second concerns the method employed to derive data for the analysis, while the third concerns the kind of issue being analyzed. Some if not all analytical approaches can be applied equally to image-based research and non-image-based research. A Marxist analysis, for example, while normally found in the study of economic and political behaviour, could be appplied to the study of images (as John Berger did in his famous study of fine art, *Ways of Seeing*, 1972). Similarly, the same methodology can be applied to both images and non-images. Content analysis, for example, which methodically and objectively assesses variable features in a set of items (see below), can be equally deployed in the analysis of magazine cover photographs or in the analysis of politicians' speeches. Finally, an issue such as the role of material objects in human social relations could be approached from a number of different analytical perspectives (Marxist, functionalist, and so on), using a number of different methodologies (content analysis, reflexivity, and so on).

In the remainder of this chapter I wish to outline a number of analytical and methodological approaches to the study of images and illustrate them with a number of examples, concentrating almost exclusively on approaches that deal with found, or pre-existing, images. The examples, however, do not by any means exhaust the possible kinds of issues that might be explored. I begin with a discussion of largely 'desk-bound' approaches to visual studies coming from the broad discipline of cultural studies; such approaches tend to rely more on persuasive argument than objective data analysis to achieve their ends. I then move on to discuss what I call more 'formalist' approaches, those that collect visual data and then subject it to distinctive and patterned forms of analysis. Following this I shift to more subjective approaches, which tend to necessitate fieldwork of some kind rather than simple 'data collection'. I conclude the chapter with some observations about image materiality, which might need to be dealt with in field situations, thus providing the transition to the following chapter.

Approaches from cultural studies and other perspectives

In later sections I will address particular forms of visual analysis (such as content analysis), but first I wish to survey a broad set of approaches towards the study of the visual that can generally be subsumed under the heading of 'cultural studies'.[10]

Themes in visual cultural studies

Although cultural studies is a distinct discipline in its own right, I use the term here more broadly to encompass approaches within the social sciences and humanities that draw upon post-structuralist theory (itself a broad term encompassing a wide variety of non-positivistic theoretical movements from gender studies, to phenomenology, to postcolonialism) to make claims about the role images play in maintaining or subverting established forms of social practice. As a relatively recent disciplinary approach, and drawing widely on a wide range of other disciplines, it offers little in the way of distinct methodology (Lister and Wells, 2001, p. 63). However, it has a relatively distinctive, if broad, subject matter and, although a highly diverse field, some common or at least overlapping sets of assumptions. One distinctive feature is to set aside a distinction between 'high' and 'low' culture (Shakespeare versus *EastEnders*, for example). Thus when it comes to what is generally known in the literature as 'visual culture', everything and anything can be considered, from billboard adverts, to art-house cinema, to the changed experience of viewing landscape with the introduction of motorized transport. Nonetheless, two leading exponents of a cultural studies approach have argued that until recently the discipline has overlooked visual culture (Evans and Hall, 1999, p. 1).

Cultural studies is concerned with the production and consumption of 'culture', primarily in a Euro-American context, and confines itself largely to the modern period and the (recent) historical antecedents of contemporary cultural forms. These forms need not have a visual component (shopping, for example) but frequently do. Jenks, drawing upon the influential work of Martin Jay (e.g. 1989, 1992), argues that the modern world 'is very much a "seen" phenomenon' (1995, p. 2). Similarly, Mirzoeff begins his book on visual culture with a written description of a cascade of the images that surround the citizens of contemporary Euro-America, particularly the many screens we look at and the many cameras that watch us (Mirzoeff, 1999, pp. 1 ff.). Finally, much writing in the discipline invokes earlier scholars who wrote extensively or in passing about vision and visual forms: Foucault, Bourdieu, Barthes, even Marx.

Ocularcentrism and the saturation of images

So if cultural studies is concerned primarily with the everyday cultural forms of contemporary Euro-American society, and if that society is oriented towards privileges, and endlessly produces 'the visual' (ocularcentrism), how can Evans and Hall claim a neglect? Their answer is that in much cultural studies literature the modes of analysis applied to visual forms and practices are essentially language-based and semiotic in approach, as with the formalist modes of analysis discussed in the previous section. Consequently, they claim, visual artefacts tend to be approached as any other cultural text with regard to their meaning, and the specific contexts of their use, production, consumption and so forth can be seen simply as another aspect of society's cultural practices (Evans and Hall, 1999, p. 2). But not only might the realm of the visual be qualitatively different, and require a different approach, the primarily linguistic models of communication that are applied are claimed to be inadequate: the goal should not merely be an exploration into the 'meaning' of the visual texts studied, but the more fundamental one of assessing society's modernist modes of creating and sustaining those 'meanings' in the first place. Seeing and knowing are mutually constitutive, the former is not a passive medium (through representation) for the latter, as the linguistic communication model would presume (Evans and Hall, 1999, p. 3; see also Mirzoeff, 1999, pp. 15–16). Others have also pointed out the problems (and their solutions) that cultural studies has with the visual, or at least to a need for a rethink of analytical assumptions.

Jenks (1995), for example, argues that the very ocularcentrism of (post)modernist Euro-America renders it difficult to think through or around it: as members of that same society, with the same historical and cultural background, we can, as it were, be blinded to vision (one possible solution to this is reflexivity, discussed below). Jenks also notes that for the same reason 'visual culture' as a category is 'almost redundant', there being a visual aspect to (almost?) all areas of cultural experience (1995, p. 16); the contributors to his edited book, he goes on to point out, all concentrate on obvious, 'tangible' forms such as cinema and advertising. In a similar fashion, Lister and Wells assert that the study of specifically visual culture is not merely a subdivision of cultural studies, but that the saturation of images and image-making technologies in contemporary society demands that the discipline of cultural studies itself should be reworked (2001, p. 62).

In these reworkings, several points are made. First, as noted above, analytical strategies that rely on linguistically derived models of semiotic communication are inadequate. One reason for this is that there is, or can be, an immediate sensory experience that comes from encountering a visual image that other forms of text cannot replicate (Mirzoeff gives the example of the spaceship filling the screen in Ken Russell's *2001: A Space Odyssey*: 1999, p. 15). It could of course be argued (e.g. van Leeuwen, 2001, p. 94) that this is merely what Barthes calls the level of denotation – what the picture is 'of' (a spaceship in this case); semiotic analysis is concerned with the second level, that of connotation (what meaning or idea is being communicated) (Barthes, 1973). More is meant than this, however; later in *2001* there are sequences of images that connote very little, as the lead character, Bowman, passes through the wormhole, and yet which are (or were in the days before CGI imagery in Hollywood films) expressive and powerful. In addition, Barthes's later notion of the 'punctum', the impact of an image, is an attempt to address this distinctive capacity of the visual, strongly linked to notions of desire (Mirzoeff, 1999, p. 16; see also Mulvey's highly influential work on desire and sexuality, e.g. 1975). What is partly at issue here is the analytical strategy of phenomenology, which I shall return to below.

Image context

The second point made in relation to the reworking of cultural studies concerns context. Several analysts point out that the context in which an image is encountered (what I would call part of its external narrative) is not merely something to be subsequently taken into account: the 'meaning' of the image and the 'meaning' of the context are mutually constituting. Taking a famous image of the French social photographer Robert Doisneau from 1948–9, 'An oblique glance', Lister and Wells show how context works (2001, pp. 67–8). The photograph is taken inside a shop, an art dealer's, looking out through the display window to the street beyond. A man and a women are standing before the window, but while she looks straight ahead at a picture, only the back of which can be seen by the photograph's viewer, the man looks obliquely across her to a painting both he and the photograph's viewer can see. This is a 'saucy' image of a naked woman from the rear. The original context of viewing was a French photo-magazine (*Pointe de Vue*). It would perhaps have raised a smile from the male reader-viewer, perhaps a tut of displeasure from his wife. It would have been seen as part of a sequence of images, representing their lives, their city, their country to themselves. A modern viewer, as Lister and Wells point out, is more likely to encounter the image in the white space of a gallery, as Doisneau's work is not only popular today, reproduced on posters, but also subject to serious academic and critical attention. It is not simply that the context has changed, the context has changed the image: this rather light-hearted image is no longer read as a then-contemporary comment on social mores, but with ironic humour, a smile raised less by the image itself than by the curator's selection of it for inclusion in the exhibition.[11]

Power and the image

Finally, some in the field of (visual) cultural studies are concerned with the material nature of the image itself, an issue that I address below. Taken together, however, all these perspectives on visual cultural studies share a number of concerns, of which perhaps the primary one is power. Like anthropology and sociology, cultural studies is concerned not only with who is doing the looking (or gazing, or controlling the circulation of images, or whatever), but whom society empowers to look and to be looked at, and with how the act of looking produces knowledge that in turn constitutes society. Such concerns are not absent from formalist approaches, but as with the issue of broader context more generally, they are seen as a subsequent stage of analysis. For cultural studies the analysis of the image and a concern with power/ knowledge (to use Foucault's phrase indicating the interconnection between the two) cannot be separated. For this analytical approach, the knowledge gained from the study of the image is produced by and goes on to produce power.

Much of the thinking about the power/knowledge aspect of the visual derives from Foucault's famous co-option of Bentham's panopticon (see the case study at the start of this chapter). John Tagg's work on the history of photography, for example, makes direct use of Foucauldian notions of panoptic surveillance and the uses of photography to produce power/knowledge about the poor, the mentally ill and the criminal in the nineteenth century (Tagg, 1987). However, Andrew Barry (1995) considers Foucault's understanding of the panopticon, and other analysts' investigations into technologies of surveillance such as city-centre CCTV recording, to be approaches that treat these technologies as 'inhuman' or automatic, their operations governed by 'society' and independent of the actual men and women who deploy them. Although Tagg and others readily supply examples of individual agents – psychiatrists, police officials, criminologists, and others – who conceptualize and implement the technologies of surveillance, the implication is that they are agents of the state, acting 'under orders' from society at large (a similar inference can be drawn from the more formalist analytical strategies discussed in the following section, with their apparent lack of concern for the creators and users of the images selected for analysis).

In his article Barry considers three categories of people – doctors, journalists and anthropologists – who have been accused of exercising 'scopic regimes' to discipline and control the bodies and lives of others. Drawing his analytical framework, ironically, from another of Foucault's contributions (*The Birth of the*

Clinic, 1973), Barry seeks to demonstrate that, possibly despite their intentions, practitioners of these three professions do interfere with the implementation of these inhuman technologies. 'Personality', 'ethics' and 'professional experience' all insert a human dimension into the inhuman practice (Barry, 1995, p. 54).

For example, the early years of my own discipline of social anthropology are associated with the colonial project of the European powers. The relationship is complex and need not be gone into here, but from a Foucauldian perspective there are certainly parallels between the colonizers' and the anthropologists' desire to 'know' the subjugated peoples. Part of that knowledge was gained through visual means – producing photographs of colonial 'types', for example, in the nineteenth century (see Chapter 2), and later the use of photographs on identity cards. But even after anthropology, from the 1920s onwards, had largely abandoned the use of photography as a scientific tool, a tension remained in ethnographic writing between scientific or objective discussion and the far more subjective opinion and comments of the ethnographer, in particular his (but sometimes her) continual reminders to the reader that he was actually there and observed what he describes. Yet both modes were, and are, accorded authority by fellow professionals.

As Barry points out, earlier generations of anthropologists were not trained in field methods but, like doctors, learned their fieldworking skills through experience and their writing skills through practice (1995, p. 53).[12] Early twentieth-century anthropologists such as Malinowski influenced the direction of the discipline not because they were passive implementers of society's scopic technologies, but because they combined professional status and what Barry calls 'personality' with such skill.

Analytically there are two possible directions to go in at this point, the choice being dictated by the researcher's underlying theoretical perspective. For those researchers concerned primarily with society's structure, the analysis simply loops back and substantivizes 'personality', 'ethics' and 'professional experience' as tools used by individuals to implement the scopic technologies; we thus return to a Foucauldian position, albeit one that has been humanized to a degree (this is essentially what Barry finally does: 1995, p. 55). The alternative direction, more palatable to those whose concern lies primarily with human agents, is an ethnomethodological (see below) theoretical underpinning that would go on to assert the cumulative actions of Malinowski and others as constitutive of the technologies of viewing, not as indicative of them.

There is a great deal more that could be said, both about Foucauldian approaches to the study of the visual and indeed about other strands within the broad field of cultural studies. What I have said so far, however, has at least established a number of well-explored themes: ocularcentrism and the pervasiveness of visual imagery, a stress on social context (albeit established from textual rather than field sources), and power. With these themes in mind, it is time to turn to some of the common analytical methods found in visual studies.

Formalist methods

Although proponents of Foucauldian approaches and other positions within a broadly cultural studies perspective are, undoubtedly, rigorous in their logic and thinking, their work can come in for criticism from a more positivist or indeed quantitative perspective: the material chosen for analysis sometimes seems to have been chosen to suit the analysis, rather than selected more objectively to form a representative sample. As I shall discuss below, however, the two approaches are not necessarily incompatible. A sample of material, or the categorization of material, can be made in a formalist and rule-governed way, and then subsequently subjected to more interpretivist analysis.

Content analysis

The discussion that immediately follows does not even begin to give a detailed account of content analysis as it is used today (for which see P. Bell, 2001, for an extremely clear, and critical, account) and it could be argued that it is simply a technique, like performing a chi-squared test, that carries no ideological bias; that is, a researcher's prior theoretical understanding of the world of social relations does not affect the implementation of the technique. I would argue that this is not in fact the case, for the reasons given below. Today, self-defined content analysis is most commonly found in the disciplines of communication studies and media studies and tends to be quantitative and subject to a variety of rules and procedures (to ensure the reliability of the coding of the content, for example). Its practitioners strive for objectivity, and the application of the analysis tends to be governed by a rather positivist approach. However, the basic principle of observing the formal properties of a set of objects – in our case, visual images – is much more widespread and is found across a wide range of disciplines (see also Gibbs, 2007).

Although the analytical strategy of content analysis only comes into formal use in the second half of the twentieth century (consolidated in Berelson, 1952, according to Ball and Smith, 1992, p. 20), the idea itself is much older. For example, the early British social anthropologist Alfred C. Haddon used a form of it in his *Evolution in Art* (1895). In this work, written after he had become interested in 'primitive' culture, but before he undertook his pioneering expedition to the Torres Strait Islands to observe a 'primitive' society at first hand (see Chapter 2), Haddon took as his theoretical basis the notion of biological evolutionism. Like many of his contemporaries, he conjectured that in order to understand complex sociocultural forms (in this case, the art of civilized societies), one should examine simpler forms supposedly to be found amongst less civilized peoples.

This conjecture, albeit in many variant forms, was dominant in the later decades of the nineteenth and early decades of the twentieth centuries, and posited that forms of social organization and social institutions 'evolved' from simpler to more complex forms over time. While the evolutionary process itself was too slow to observe, different societies around the world were thought to display – for reasons that were never fully explained – different 'periods' of this (unilineal) process, and so by sampling social or cultural forms from a variety of them, one could build up a pseudo-historical account of the process. Haddon conjectured that just as religious ideas or kinship organization evolved over time, so too would artistic – or more particularly, decorative stylistic features – evolve. Thus Haddon's theoretical presumption was social evolutionary. His method of analysis was to sample a wide variety of decorative and other stylistic features from the material culture of 'primitive' and ancient societies. And his conclusion, a confirmation of the hypothesis, was that artistic form did indeed evolve, stemming usually from either an element in nature (such as a plant form) or from a functional object (such as a fishing hook).

While it is obvious that Haddon was interested in the content of the images,[13] hence my justification for discussing his work in this section, it is also important to consider what he was less interested in. Principally, he was weak in method, at least by today's standards. Although he had a background in science, having been trained as a marine biologist, he did not seek to quantify his findings in any way, and indeed he tells the reader almost nothing about his sampling process. The largely typological approach taken by both natural and social sciences at this time is probably explanation for this, so while the study is formalist (in the nominal sense of being concerned with form), grounded in theory and draws upon a particular analytical methodology, it is not especially robust. Despite warning the reader on several occasions to be vigilant not to search for examples to illustrate a theory (e.g. 1895, p. 11), he sometimes seems to be in danger of doing exactly that.

Content analysis of photographs   Similar points to the above are made by Ball and Smith (1992) in their assessment of content analysis approaches to visual data. Reviewing two studies of fashion based upon secondary sources such as magazine illustrations and paintings of women's dress (Richardson and Kroeber, 1940) and men's beards (Robinson, 1976), they show some of the strengths and weaknesses of the approach. One strength is the finding that changing fashions in both dress and beard style appear to follow a century-long cycle (Ball and Smith, 1992, pp. 24–5). That is, over the course of a half century, styles of dress and beard shifted until they reached the opposite state – widest to narrowest width of skirt, pervasive to rare occurrences of beard – and then began the reverse process over the next half century. While one might intuitively have a sense of this from one's own observation of the world, or in this case historical illustrations, the strength of the two pieces of research is to validate – or possibly contradict – one's initial impression. But there are weaknesses too. First, although both studies employ a defined sampling frame to source the images for analysis,

Richardson and Kroeber acknowledge that their data sources are varied and increasingly arbitrary the further back in the period (1605–1936) they go. Hence, although the analysis is quantitative (unlike that of Haddon), inevitable bias in data selection may be distorting the findings. Robinson's study is more robust in this regard: images of men with and without facial hair taken from a single source, the *Illustrated London News*. Secondly, the category choices and the subsequent coding procedures could be open to additional bias. Ball and Smith work through these problems with admirable clarity (1992, pp. 23–7) and as a non-quantitative researcher myself, I am less interested in these technical issues than with what seems to be a more fundamental problem.

While, as Ball and Smith note, the findings of both studies appear to show 'evidence of a supraindividual cultural patterning of changes in fashion, a patterning that cannot be accounted for by stock psychological explanations of imitation, emulation, and competition'[14] (1992, p. 25), crucially absent is a consideration of context and meaning. By context, I mean asking questions such as 'Why were these portraits of women painted?', or 'Why did the *Illustrated London News* select these photographs for publication, and not others?' Such questions are still essentially questions of sampling; presumably other historical sources could be consulted to confirm or deny the representativeness of the samples taken. But questions of meaning still remain; in contemporary India, for example, my own visual experience, supported by questioning people on the matter, tells me that for men who constitute a vast swathe of the society (Hindus) the issue of beard/not-beard is a marker firstly of layman versus holy man or monk (*sadhu*), and secondly of Hindu versus Muslim and Sikh. That is, while there may well be historical fluctuations of a regular, cyclical type of the kind Robinson observes for English society, the fact is that, in the past few decades at least, beards (though not moustaches) are largely correlated with religious affiliation.

Manifest and latent content Ball and Smith address this last point rather differently, as an issue of reading manifest versus latent content. For coding to be reliable, coding procedures need to be objectively and unambiguously applicable. Hence researchers read what Ball and Smith term the 'manifest' content of the image (a man with facial hair) and then make a note of the type of facial hair (full beard, mutton-chop whiskers, etc.); what is ignored is the symbolic or 'latent' content: the meaning of mutton-chop whiskers in 1910, or full beards in India, or whatever. But at a more abstract level of analysis, one could argue that the 'latent' content of the images, or at least the entire set of images, is precisely the 'evidence of a supraindividual cultural patterning' at work, a reading that is unavailable to both the men with facial hair and perhaps to the researcher until she performs the analysis and sees the pattern emerge. By contrast, for the owners of the beards at certain periods, and perhaps too for the picture editors of the

Illustrated London News who selected those images for publication, the manifest content would indeed include the symbolic associations (these are fashionable men). It is partly for this reason that I find distinctions between manifest and latent content to be less than satisfactory, and prefer instead my distinction between internal and external narratives combined with the notion of perspective (see Chapter 1), which makes the relationship between actors, including the social researcher, more clear.

As noted at the start of this section, readers should turn elsewhere for a detailed 'how to' guide to using content analysis (P. Bell, 2001, is recommended), but the argument is generally made, either critically or as a mere statement of fact, that discussions of meaning are either ignored or deliberately set on one side. Content analysis and other formalist analytical strategies are therefore often used as a precursor analytical strategy to another form of analysis. In the case of Haddon's work on stylistic and decorative forms, the overarching form of analysis was social evolutionary theory, for example. Ball and Smith discuss French anthropologist Claude Lévi-Strauss's well-known analysis of Northwest Coast Native American masks (Lévi-Strauss, 1983) as a classic structuralist interpretation of visual representation, and this too relies on an assessment or analysis of content, in this case stylistic features of the masks such as bulging eyes.

Perhaps the most common analytical frame allied with content analysis is some form of semiotic analysis. As with Lévi-Straussian structuralism, much semiotic analysis derives from a base in linguistics and sometimes the arcane debates over the meaning of terminology can seem almost theological; Kress and van Leeuwen (1996) provide a brief overview in the course of outlining their own position of 'social semiotics' (1996, pp. 5 ff.). Semiotic approaches, social or otherwise, do not themselves always constitute the complete extent of the analysis. Jewitt and Oyama note that the analysis is 'not an end in itself' (2001, p. 136). They go on to describe how in a piece of research analyzing the composition, spatial relationships, geometry, etc., of visual materials used in sexual health campaigns, Jewitt's use of content analysis/social semiotics codified and systematized data could then be interpreted by theories of gender and sexuality.

Content analysis of film When such perspectives are applied to film (or videotape) rather than sampled collections of still images, the rhythm of the editing as well as the presence of speech and music must also be taken into account, complicating the process considerably. In an article analyzing an Australian documentary film about the problems of delivering health care effectively in a hospital, Iedema (2001) systematically notes several features about the film (such as the positioning of subjects relative to the camera) to come to the conclusion that whatever the 'manifest' content of the film might be (in the sense used by Ball and Smith, above), an analysis of the film's latent content shows that it is the medical clinicians (rather than, say, the patients or the administrators) who have the most privileged voice (2001, p. 200). Iedema's account is undoubtedly thorough, to the point of acknowledging several shortcomings with the approach (2001, pp 200–1). Two of these are essentially different sides of the same coin: the views, opinions and experiential context of neither the film's creators nor the film's (intended) viewers can find any place in the analysis. Herein lies one of the difficulties of focusing – following Durkheim, Marx, Saussure and Lévi-Strauss amongst others – on hidden ('latent') meanings that transcend or are completely unavailable to those who are performing the social action. Not only can it be anti-humanistic (which is a moral rather than a methodological objection), like most if not all forms of formalist analysis there is a certain inevitability to it: criteria are set that define data, the data so produced are subjected to a formal and carefully bounded process, and a result is produced.

A further difficulty with such approaches is that they can be inflexible; for example, in the more heavily quantitative applications of content analysis it is vital to ensure that coders of content do not change their minds or refine the categories halfway through the process. Of course, if a researcher did decide after partially coding a series of news photographs for, say, instances of masculine violence, that it might make a difference if she included subcategories indicating the gender of the person(s) to whom the violence was directed, then presumably she could start all over again. But what is to ensure that the same thing wouldn't happen once more? However, there is one form of still relatively formalist analysis that does build in iterative re-examination from the start. Commonly known as grounded theory and deriving from a work of the same name by Glaser and Strauss (1967), the approach can also sometimes be the subject of arcane doctrinal discussions, but at its simplest is a formalization of a principle already mentioned – that theory, or perhaps more accurately analysis, and investigation are in a dialectical relationship, with each influencing the other (see Ball, 1998, p. 133). An example of grounded theory being used in visual research, but in a purely qualitative context, is discussed in the next chapter.

There is a great deal more that could be said about the approaches described above, but I hope I have given enough detail to indicate the broad perspectives. One thing such formalist approaches have in common is that, while not strictly quantitative methodologies, they are amenable to and often employ quantitative methods in their execution. Whilst these may range from simply counting and tabulating to more sophisticated tests of significance, all have the effect of further formalizing these forms of analysis. To the supporters of formalist analysis the inclusion of quantitative methods provides increased guarantees of robustness and reliability; those less enamoured see rigidity, inflexibility and oversimplification. However, as the subject matter of this book is qualitative, not quantitative, methodology, I have little further to say about this, though I return to issues of robustness in Chapter 6 (see more about analyzing qualitative data in Gibbs, 2007).

Ethnomethodology

Ethnomethodology is largely to be found in sociology departments, but it is a wide-ranging approach and practitioners are found in a variety of disciplines. Again, there is no space here to discuss the discipline fully, or even to summarize it adequately (ten Have, 2004, is a good recent introduction and of methodological relevance and also Rapley, 2007), but at its core is the study of the everyday methodologies by which people achieve successful social interaction. One large area of interest has been natural language and conversation (as opposed to formal grammar), for example the ways in which people judge how to take turns in a conversation, or 'repair' a conversation that has gone awry for some reason. There are, however, some examples of ethnomethodological approaches to and uses of visual materials.

At the end of their short but incisive survey of visual analysis, Ball and Smith briefly discuss ethnomethodological approaches to visual analysis (1992, pp. 61–7). They take as their examples several studies of science practice, particularly astronomy, to demonstrate that physicists use images to create the phenomena they study, while at the same time the physicists believe – from their positivistic standpoint – that the phenomena they study (pulsars in this case) are 'out there' independent of their study. The aim of the ethnomethodological studies cited is not to relativize laboratory science (though this is possibly an outcome) but simply to demonstrate one of the discipline's core tenets, that experience of the world constitutes knowledge of that world through an iterative process. By a process of close observation, ethnomethodologists uncover the routine everyday practices – methods – by which people order their lives, in this case their professional lives. Strictly speaking, the studies cited by Ball and Smith are not ethnomethodological studies of visual systems but rather studies of working practice, part of which involves those observed, rather than the researchers, using images.

Some ethnomethodological studies, however, take a more obviously visual approach. For example, Heath and Hindmarsh (2002) describe how they have used video to record doctor/patient interactions, which are then analyzed using an expanded form of conversation analysis that pays attention to looks and gestures, as well as to speech.[15] Video has also been used as a data-capturing method for classic ethnomethodological topics such as how people select seats on a train, or negotiate crossing the road at busy pedestrian intersections (ten Have, 2004, p. 158). Even at this point there can be differences in initial orientation, however. Heath and Hindmarsh, for example, placed their camera to get as much in the frame as possible – situated to observe the faces and bodies of the doctor and patients and using a wide-angle lens. The camera's position therefore is that of the observer, superfluous to the social interaction being observed. Ten Have, however, gives the example of a self-initiated methodological shift on the part of one his students, which shifts the camera from an observer standpoint to a participant standpoint. Replicating a famous earlier study of a pedestrian crossing, the student initially filmed from a high vantage point where she could see all the people equally. But as Livingston, the author of the original study, pointed out, none of the pedestrians can see from this vantage point and therefore cannot be employing this 'knowledge' to negotiate their passage through the crowd. Consequently the student placed the camera in a bag on her shoulder and filmed again, this time as a participant in the crowd, and sought to gain experiential visual 'knowledge' of the action (ten Have, 2004, p. 159).

Goodwin notes that 'for the past thirty years both conversation analysis and ethnomethodology have provided extensive analysis of how human vision is socially constructed', but then goes on to note that in fact many of these studies 'are not analyses of representations or vision *per se* but instead the part played by visual phenomena in the production of meaningful action' (2001, p. 157). Of course, a version of the same statement could be made for most if not all of the analytical strategies described so far in this chapter; as stated in Chapter 1, the goal of social research is to learn about society and visual methods are a route to that goal, not an end in themselves. However, many of the analytical strategies mentioned so far involve some kind of examination of the ontology of the image itself, while some ethnomethodological studies seem untroubled by this. Goodwin, however, provides examples of studies where the image or object of vision is recognized to be fluid in its representational powers, dependent upon what he calls the multiple 'semiotic fields' within which it is located and encountered (2001, p. 164); he also recognizes the potential importance of a visual object's material status or properties, a point I address below (see Rapley, 2007, for more details).

Reflexivity and other experiential approaches

I mentioned above that ten Have's student sought to understand the behaviour of a crowd of pedestrians at a traffic intersection by experiencing the crowd herself (and videotaping her passage through the crowd). My own discipline of social anthropology has, in recent years, particularly stressed the idea of subjective and experiential understandings of social action, something that is really only possible to investigate in field contexts (discussed in the next chapter). It is, however, possible to introduce the idea at this stage, and particularly the central notion of reflexivity.

The term is used to indicate the researcher's awareness of her own self, the conduct of her research, and the response to her presence; that is, the researcher recognizes and evaluates her own actions as well as those of others.[16] Within some recent anthropological work, including visual anthropological analysis, this has come to be a key methodological practice. As Pink points out, this is not simply a question of noting and eliminating bias (2001, p. 19) so that positivist objectivity can be restored. Rather, the reflexive approach rests on a theoretical development in anthropology and other disciplines that create (written) ethnographic representation.

In the mid-1980s, what has come to be known as 'the crisis of representation'[17] caused anthropologists to examine the modes by which the authority of an ethnographic account was created and sustained, given that strategies deployed in other areas of social research – surveys generating statistical evidence in sociology, for example, or extensive transcripts of conversations in conversation analysis – were little used. Tools derived from literary criticism were used to show how certain stylistic devices or literary models created the air of authority that earlier ethnographic writings rested upon: ethnography, as Edmund Leach (1989) declared towards the end of his life, is fiction . By 'fiction', of course, is meant the idea that written ethnographies – the particular problems associated with filmed ethnographies will be discussed in the next chapter – are constructed accounts, with authors, not transparent and objective descriptions of the lives of others.

The more nihilistic response to the 'crisis' was to declare that anthropology was over, as its core practices – long-term participant-observation fieldwork and ethnographic writing – were now seen to be fatally compromised. Rather more positive solutions included the suggestion that anthropologists should publish their field notes and any other associated documents along with their ethnographies – an idea that would be unlikely to interest publishers, but which will be taken up again in Chapter 5.

Another, and in many ways related idea, was that of reflexivity. By the author examining herself, and taking notice of how others respond to her not only as an individual person but within the context of race, class, gender, and forth, and by communicating those understandings to the reader, the reader would have a greater opportunity to position the text, to understand the viewpoint or perspective of the ethnographer. Pink (2001), provides a number of specifically anthropological examples of this in her book on visual methodologies as does Chaplin (1994) with regard to sociology. In fact, such reflexivity need not be associated with the further shores of the postmodernist ocean. As Ruby pointed out in an article originally published in 1980, a clear description of the methodological processes involved is a routine element in academic science papers (how many grams of which chemicals were mixed, what temperature the mixture was heated to, etc.) and a reflexive approach in the human sciences is merely one that acknowledges the investigator herself as a 'tool' by which the research is conducted (Ruby, 2000, chap. 6).

There are several other perspectives and analytical strategies that invoke subjectivity or in other ways develop and extend the principle of reflexivity in visual research – phenomenology (see Stoller, 1989, on learning to 'see' in Niger), action research (a variant of grounded theory), drawing upon one's past training and skill in a fine-art field (see Ramos, 2004, on producing paintings for a display at an

Ethiopian research institute), psychoanalysis and imagework (see Diem-Wille 2001; Edgar 2004) – but all rely on empirical research and interaction with the research subjects and so are dealt with in the next chapter. Instead the next section briefly considers not so much an analytical perspective, but the consequence of an observation: visual representations are often material artefacts.

Image materiality

Before concluding this chapter, I wish to introduce one final idea before moving on to fieldwork practices. Strictly speaking, materiality is a property of visual objects that can be studied, rather than an analytical or methodological approach as such. However, if consideration is given to the material properties of visual things prior to embarking upon their study in the field (or indeed thinking about them in the office), then the shape of the study may well be altered.

From the work of Lister and Wells (2001) I have already given a brief example of how the context in which an image is viewed might alter understandings of how it is 'read'. While this is often linked analytically to the possibilities that 'reproducibility' offers (Evans and Hall, 1999, p. 3), it can also be linked to the material properties of the reproduction.

Similar to the distinction between external and internal narratives in the reading of images, it is important for the social researcher to distinguish between the *form* of a visual image and the *content* of a visual image. While linked, form and content are at least analytically separable and it is often helpful to consider the extent to which form dictates or mediates content. In all cases of mechanical image production and reproduction, such as video and still or moving photography, as well as in many non-mechanical cases, the material characteristics of the form serve to shape or even constrain the possible content. Conversely, through paint or other non-mechanical media it is possible to represent both those things that can be seen with the naked eye and those that cannot (but see Latour, 1988, on the rise of scientific rationalism and the consequent difficulty of representing 'heaven' in religious painting).

The relationship between form and content is not fixed of course and attention should be paid to the extent – if any – to which one is privileged over the other in any particular social context. Attention paid to the materiality of the visual image, and the materiality of its context, can serve to illuminate the distinctive texture of social relations in which it is performing its work. Until they were banned altogether, billboard advertisements for cigarettes could not be displayed in the near proximity of schools, for example, while the presence or absence of photographic images and other non-textual visual elements can serve to distinguish one newspaper from another (Kress and van Leeuwen nicely contrast the front page of *The Sun*, a British tabloid, with that of the *Frankfurter Allgemeine Zeitung*, a German broadsheet: 1996, pp. 28–9).

Materiality and 'The Cornfield'

Some researchers have used the form versus content distinction to problematize the 'meaning' ascribed to a visual image. For example, Chaplin (1998) writes about an exhibition at the National Gallery in London, which focused on a single painting, John Constable's *The Cornfield* (1826). Prior to the exhibition, the organizer and staff of the Gallery used notices in a local newspaper and next to the painting itself in the Gallery to find members of the public who had reproductions of the painting in their homes. Some of these reproductions then became part of the exhibition, together with a videotape in which people described what the painting (or their reproduction thereof) meant to them (Chaplin, 1998, pp. 303–4). The selected reproductions were in a variety of media but were typically utilitarian objects decorated with a reproduction of part or whole of the painting: tea towels, plates, firescreens, thimbles, clocks, wallpaper.

One of Chaplin's findings was that some of the 45 people who answered the newspaper advertisement 'were unaware of the existence of the original painting and had never heard of John Constable' (Chaplin, 1998, p. 303). The domestic objects, even if not used for their functional purpose but displayed ornamentally (as doubtless the decorated plates and thimbles were), were part of an assemblage of material items within the home that conveyed meaning in conversation with one another, and with their owners and their visitors. Vague yet comforting associations of a golden rural past, of leisure and days out in the country, of childhood innocence, triggered by the reproduced content of the known or unidentified original painting are combined with the class and status imperatives to maintain a nice, well-ordered and well-decorated home triggered by the material form, existence and display of the decorated objects. It is the consumption of material goods and their decorative content that would appear to give meaning to these visual artefacts, not merely their association with what Alfred Gell has called 'the art cult' (Gell, 1992, p. 42; see also Gell, 1998, pp. 62–4, 97).

In this example the material forms of the Constable reproduction place their owners in a particular relation to the art world (Becker, 1982) that gives the painting meaning, even if this place is rather peripheral prior to the 1996 exhibition. Chaplin, however, does not discuss how these visual images stand in relation to other visual images in their homes, nor how they mediate or represent relationships between their owners and others in their more immediate social environment (see Rapley, 2007, on discourse analysis).

Photographic display

The place of objects in the home is addressed by David Morley, who cites a number of studies to show that domestic television sets frequently act as a dual medium for the display of visual images, as there is a common tendency to place a variety of physical objects on top of the set, but especially photographs, the viewer thus receiving two images for the price of one as it were (Morley, 1995, pp. 182 ff.). In

Euro-America the photographs displayed on the top of television sets are commonly family photographs, very often studio portraits or at least posed pictures representing important life-cycle events, as opposed to holiday snapshots, which tend to be hidden away for more intimate consumption in albums. Form is generally secondary to content in such images, and to some extent the television set top acts as a kind of shrine for the display of a family's significant images and other objects such as china ornaments and holiday souvenirs, the bounded and pier-like surface acting as a more suitable space than a run of shelves or another item of furniture that is already designed to hold objects, such as a table or sideboard. Mantelpieces, in homes that have them, may serve a similar shrine-like function. Yet if it is a shrine there is generally no special relevance accorded to pictures of the dead, in marked contrast to photographic displays elsewhere.

In India, away from the metropolitan centres, family photographs are rarely displayed on a television set. More particularly, photographs of the living are also rarely on show in any context, but are generally confined to albums (the ubiquitous wedding album) or tucked away in their envelopes in drawers or boxes. Photographs of the dead, however, are frequently displayed. Normally, these are photographs taken in life, sometimes explicitly taken in middle or old age with the aim of being used subsequently as memorial images. Pinney cites examples of existing wedding or other photographs being reworked for memorial representation where no other image exists; he also cites cases of post-mortem photographs being taken by family or studio professionals and used as the basis of a retouched memorial image (Pinney, 1997, pp. 139, 205).

In most of these cases the materiality of the image is marked, sometimes quite literally. In relatively wealthier urban homes I have visited in western India, where access to studio portrait photography was possible during the past few decades, a standard practice is to enlarge a studio photograph of the deceased person in the prime of life, sometimes to have it hand coloured, and then to frame and hang it prominently on the wall. In Hindu homes it is common to hang a garland of fresh or artificial flowers around the frame of the image on the anniversary of the death of the person. Incense may be burned in front of such photographs, and the foreheads of those represented may be dotted with vermilion or sandalwood paste. Photographic images of the dead, intermingled with photographic and artistic representations of sacred places and persons, can also be found away from the domestic context, in the meeting halls of religious groups and caste communities for example (where the dead will be revered religious or community leaders). In cases such as these the content of the images is obviously important, but so too is the material form around and upon which social acts are performed. In the domestic context there is little or no cultural space for a 'mere' photograph of a living family member.

Object, analysis and method

While not strictly an analytical strategy, a consideration given to the material properties of images – including the mere fact of their material existence – can help ground many of the analytical strategies discussed in this chapter in an empirical context. There are of course many other positions and strategies that can and have been informed by visual analysis in sociological research. However, the aim of this chapter has been to give an indication of some of the more common positions with regard to the analysis of pre-existing images. In the next chapter I turn to the main focus of this book, the methodology of visual research in the field, which involves the creation as well as the analysis of images. But before getting to that, an assessment of the modes of analysis discussed might be called for: How should the social researcher choose between them? Is it possible to identify particular research strategies – right from the inception of a project, through its execution, to completion and dissemination – that are somehow 'better' or 'worse' than others?[18] The brief answer is 'no', at least not in absolute terms. Certainly from my own analytical perspective, it is hard to say that some particular strategy or mode of analysis is fundamentally wrong or right. Despite my claim at the start of this chapter that theory and method are inextricably intertwined, just how that intertwining takes place is, ultimately, the choice of the social researcher, the minimum requirement simply being one of consistency. Therefore, the following chapter presents a variety of methods adopted by visual social researchers, with little explicit discussion of the theory that might inform these approaches. In a spirit of eclecticism and open inquiry the researcher is encouraged to think for herself, to consider these methods and their epistemological foundations, and to think carefully about those she might wish to adopt, and why.

Key points

- Euro-American society is saturated with visual imagery: an interesting thought experiment for a researcher is to try to imagine what their chosen area of study would 'look' like if all visual forms were removed. This should then help a researcher to identify what, if anything, the visual imagery is adding.
- Images, even those created by the researcher, should always be considered in context, in particular the contexts of production, consumption and exchange. While a researcher's particular project may focus on only one of these in detail, she should nonetheless think through the other contexts.
- While of course close attention should be paid to the content of images, the material form in which images are encountered is often

equally important. Again, as a thought experiment, researchers might like to imagine what effect a change in the material form of the images they are studying could cause to the analysis; for example, would a sequence of still photographs 'work' better than a short sequence of videotape?

Further reading

Gillian Rose's book provides a very clear introduction to non-field-based forms of visual analysis, as does the first half of Emmison and Smith's book. Both are textbooks, containing exercises. Victoria Alexander provides a more concise overview in a volume that contains other important chapters on (non-visual) qualitative research. Evans and Hall (1999) and Mirzoeff (1999) are both often-cited collections of essays from a broadly cultural studies perspective, but Souza's review of both volumes highlights important differences between the two. Gibbs provides an overview of qualitative data analysis, while Rapley gives an overview of discourse and conversation analysis.

Alexander, V. (2001) 'Analysing visual materials', in N. Gilbert (ed.), *Researching Social life*. London: Sage, pp. 343–57.

de Souza, L.M.T.M. (2002) 'Review of: Jessica Evans and Stuart Hall (eds), *Visual Culture: The Reader*. London: Sage, 1999 and Nicholas Mirzoeff (ed.), *The Visual Culture Reader*. London: Routledge, 1998', *Visual Communication*, 1: 129–36.

Emmison, M. and Smith, P. (2000) *Researching the Visual: Images, Objects, Contexts and Interactions in Social and Cultural Enquiry*. London: Sage.

Gibbs, G. (2007) *Analyzing Qualitative Data*. (Book 6 of *The SAGE Qualitative Research Kit*). London: Sage.

Rose, G. (2001) *Visual Methodologies: An Introduction to the Interpretation of Visual Materials*. London: Sage.

Rapley, T. (2007) *Doing Conversation, Discourse and Document Analysis* (Book 7 of *The SAGE Qualitative Research Kit*). London: Sage.

4
Visual methods and field research

Chapter objectives
After reading this chapter, you should

- know a variety of visual methods employed during fieldwork;
- understand more about the agenda of collaboration between researcher and research subjects; and
- be aware of typical ethical concerns in visual research.

Box 4.1   Fieldwork and ethnography

All social science disciplines have some tradition of fieldwork, of researchers leaving the office and the library to gather empirical material through direct interaction with research subjects. This can range from the relatively brief and focused (a few mornings spent observing doctor/patient interactions in a surgery, for example) to the protracted and wide-ranging (two years spent living with a group of nomadic cattle-herders). While some fieldwork, particularly that oriented towards quantitative research, may involve the relatively straightforward administration of questionnaires or other pro-formas, visual methods are more likely to be employed in more complex field interactions. Alongside interviews and surveys, the most common fieldwork methodological practice is ethnography. Originally the sole preserve of social anthropology, the use of the

(Continued)

(Continued)

ethnographic method has come to be common in many if not all social science disciplines, although different things are meant by the term. In some forms of research 'ethnography' simply means observation of people's natural behaviour in their own environment, away from the artificial environment of a laboratory or other setting to which the research subjects have been invited. For many social anthropologists, however, it means far more than this, entailing an engagement with people's lives that may ultimately be lifelong, and which certainly involves complex, many-layered social encounters and obligations.

FIGURE 4.1   Paul Henley and Georges Drion filming a parade for the feast of San Juan in Cuyagua, Venezuela. Through visual ethnographic exploration, the importance of the saint to the black population of Venezuela's Caribbean coast is made clear (photograph by Dominique Nedelka, Courtesy of Paul Henley)

Ethnographic fieldwork tends to be holistic, seeking to understand all aspects of peoples' lives as a whole; even if the focus of a study is on some particular aspect of life, for example economic behaviour, this is still understood within the broader context of their life experiences and social environment. Ethnographic fieldwork tends also to seek an understanding of what people actually do, as opposed to what they say they do, or what the 'rules' of society might say they should do. Finally, ethnographic fieldwork aims to investigate tacit knowledge – those things that people know yet that they do not consciously know that they know. How, for example, do people in contemporary Britain 'know' how to take a 'good' photograph, that is, one that is recognized as such by their peers? Extensive long-term ethnographic fieldwork allows the social researcher the chance to employ a number of different methodologies in the course of their investigation, from formal interview techniques – perhaps to elicit what people say – through to observation

(Continued)

(Continued)

and video recording – to see what people do. Visual methodologies tend, on the whole, to be more exploratory than others and therefore accord with the inquiring spirit of ethnographic investigation (see also Angrosino, 2007).

Visual methods in the field

In surveying the content of this book at the end of Chapter 1, I provided a rationale for placing the previous chapter, on visual analysis, before this chapter on visual research methodology. The rationale was simply that before embarking on 'data collection', a researcher needs a sense of what she plans to do with the data subsequently. But there is another aspect too. Many of the analytical strategies described in the previous chapter, especially the more formalist ones, pertain to the analysis of found images, not created by the researcher, such as advertising images. In some cases, such as Robinson's analysis (1976) of photographs of men's facial hair in photographs printed in the *Illustrated London News*, the integrity of the investigation would have been severely compromised if the magazine's photo editors had had any inkling that such an investigation might take place, thus biasing their selection of photographs for publication. In contrast, the focus of this chapter is on the methods, and analytical justifications, by which researchers might create images in 'real-life' fieldwork situations or cause members of society to reflect upon images.[19]

Strictly speaking, there are few if any particularly distinctive or new methods of visual data collection, and it is perhaps more accurate to speak of adding a visual dimension to conventional methods of data collecting, or accentuating those that are already present. For example, the techniques of film and photo-elicitation, discussed below, are really ways of extending the standard sociological methods of interviewing. While the methods described may add to or indeed significantly alter the course of a conventional interview, many if not all of the issues discussed in companion volumes of *The SAGE Qualitative Research Kit* (e.g. Kvale, 2007; Barbour, 2007) remain pertinent. At the same time, it must be noted that visual images are not the only stimuli that can be introduced into an interview; museum ethnographers, for example, may well use objects rather than images to provoke responses from informants.

As discussed in the previous chapter, the analytical orientation of the researcher may well dictate the nature of field research conducted – if any. A brief foray to gather data, for subsequent content analysis, may require little time and little or no interaction with human subjects; for example, photographing a representative sample of graffiti for a project on space and urban youth identity. Alternatively, a project on television spectatorship and gender construction predicated on a reflexively oriented interpretivist approach to social life might devote comparatively little time to actual television viewing and a great deal to informal conversation about television viewing in pubs and office canteens. One of the strengths of visual methodologies in particular lies in the inevitably open-ended nature of the inquiry. Resisting single interpretations, images can give rise to a range of alternative paths of inquiry. Elsewhere I have discussed how an initially casual interest in the designs on Indian embroideries led me, through interviews with male and female informants, to fresh insights into marriage strategies, migration and gender ideologies, despite the fact that I had been discussing these topics with these informants over a number of years (Banks, 2001, pp. 73–9). I return to the exploratory and revelatory character of visual methodologies at the end of Chapter 6.

Photo-elicitation and other methods using found images

Before moving on to the details of photo-elicitation and other methods, it is worth re-emphasizing that images encountered in the field[20] are objects, or are encountered within a material context. As a consequence, such objects can be said to have biographies (Appadurai, 1986) in the sense that they have previous entanglements with the lives of people, which may prove important to their current roles in society when encountered by the researcher.[21] Using archival photographs to prompt memories or comments from informants in the course of an interview, for example, involves an appreciation of at least three social embeddings, or frames.

First, there is the context of original production. Perhaps a photographer visited a small rural community in the early years of this century and took a number of images. She or he could have been a middle-class metropolitan traveller on holiday using their new camera to record picturesque views and images of quaint rustics, or a government official documenting the village and its surroundings for possible future military strategy and planning purposes, or an itinerant professional photographer with a mobile studio hoping to take and then sell back some portraits of the locals. Then there is the context of the photographs' subsequent histories. Perhaps they or the negatives remained together in a trunk in an attic, or in a cupboard in a shop – with or without identifying labels – to be eventually sold at auction, donated to a picture library or archive, split up among family members, until at some point they or their copies came into the possession of the social researcher. Both these frames serve to edit the corpus of photographs. First, the original photographs represent a finite part of the infinity of all possible photographs that could have been taken on that occasion, and even that finite part is probably only a subset of all the photographs taken that did not come out, or were damaged in processing and discarded. Second, in its subsequent history a photographic collection may have been split up for sale, or an archive accepted only the part that was considered relevant to its collection policy, or all photographs of a notorious black sheep were subsequently destroyed by a family. Thus when the third frame is considered – the context in which the social researcher deploys the photographs in the course of an interview – the images' previous embeddings influence what happens next, the shadowy hand of all previous social embeddings hovers over the current one.

Watching television

Although it does not have to be, perhaps the most 'passive' form of visual field research involves watching people watching television and then interviewing them about it afterwards: film (or television) elicitation. It is passive in two senses: first, the researcher has little if any control over the images being viewed; secondly, in some cases the research may consist of little more than observation, though it is usually combined with some form of questioning. While television output can itself be the object of study (the focus of media studies approaches), I am primarily concerned in this section with research strategies that include the consumption of television programmes as an aspect of a broader social research project, rather than as an end in itself.

Such an approach means considering the context within which television is consumed. For example, James Lull advocates an approach that he describes as 'ethnographic', by which he means that researchers should spend between three and five days living with a family in their home and taking notes on television programme choice, discussions over television programmes, the degree to which the television is actually watched as opposed to providing background noise for other activities, and so forth (Lull, 1990, pp. 174 ff.). For one project, Lull sent trained undergraduate students into 85 homes in a Southern Californian town for two days to conduct this kind of 'ethnographic' observation, followed by a structured interview session on the third day in order to investigate the social uses of television, such as a substitute for education or to help in problem-solving (1990, pp. 51–60). Lull advocates this kind of approach for a number of reasons, not least the fact that the two days of observation facilitated a far higher degree of trust and co-operation from the research subjects than would be the case if the researchers had 'cold-called' with a questionnaire. Lull notes, as have many other social researchers, that gaining access to the heart of a Euro-American family for a prolonged period is no simple matter, whatever the nature of the research, and the refusal rate is high. For this reason, constructing a viable random or stratified sample from a voters' list, electoral role or telephone book is unlikely to be successful. Like others, Lull advocates approaching neighbourhood organizations, establishing trust with them (which may involve clearing and possibly modifying the research) and then contacting their members with the approval and support of the organization (1990, p. 175).

Lull also briefly discusses what one might call remote surveillance techniques of research: installing cameras and microphones into homes (with the knowledge and consent of the families involved) to record every last detail of viewing practice (1990, pp. 164, 177). Sociological and psychological studies such as this have revealed what most of us already know from our own experience: that most Euro-Americans spend a great deal of time not watching television when it is on. Peter Collett, a psychologist who employed set-top cameras for observation, in fact demonstrated that those who spend most time physically in front of the set, spent least time actually looking at the screen (cited in Lull, 1990, p. 164; see also Root, 1986, pp. 25–6). Following on from this, Morley has indicated that television should be considered primarily as an audio medium with pictures. Morley cites his own work as well as that of others to confirm that an apparently simple question from a researcher – 'What do you like to watch on television?' – has no simple answer. 'Do you mean sitting down watching?' responded one woman from Morley's own sample. 'Sitting down watching' for this woman and – one assumes – for many other women was a rare occurrence. More typically, she would be *listening* to the television from the kitchen, only coming into the room where the television was for an occasional glance at the screen (Morley, 1995, p. 174).

While considering the broader context of viewing practice, the work of Morley and Lull, at least in these cited instances, is still primarily concerned with television itself, rather than with social life more generally within which television viewing is just a part. An anthropologist in particular would have difficulty with Lull's 'ethnographic' approach. Typically, an anthropologist would be conducting broad-range ethnographic inquiries in a town or village over the course of many months, during which time she could choose to spend some time observing television-viewing practice. Such observation might be unstructured, the anthropologist simply taking notes whenever she visits a home coincided with television viewing and then ameliorating the results later, or she could adopt a standard sampling method, visiting a random or stratified sample of homes in the community at set times over a period of a month or more. Either way, the trust and familiarity that Lull speaks of would already have been established through the course of ongoing residence in the community and normal techniques of participant-observation, and would not be tied specifically into the television-viewing practice study.

Watching television in Egypt   Such an approach is exemplified in Abu-Lughod's anthropological study of television consumption in Egypt – or rather, Abu-Lughod's study of modernity in Egypt, one part of which was concerned with television (1995). She examines both the content of and the viewer response to a popular television serial, *Hilmiyya Nights*. Broadcast for five years from the late 1980s, the serial charted the relationships between two wealthy men and their families from the Cairo neighbourhood of Hilmiyya over the course of half a century. It was not, however, intended by its producers as a soap opera (where the narrative is normally driven by the interpersonal relationships of the characters) but was intended to be didactic, using the story of the characters' lives to inform the viewers about Egypt's post-Second World War political history and to promote an ideal of national unity (1995, p. 196). This is not necessarily how Abu-Lughod's informants understood it, however. Although she interviewed the programme's makers and other individuals in the Egyptian television industry to gain a sense of the serial's intentions, she was already conducting fieldwork in a village near Luxor in Upper Egypt, several hundred kilometres from the capital, Cairo. In addition, she also interviewed female domestic workers in Cairo.

Her chief conclusion from this research is that the social and political importance of the serial was more a construction of its producers than a perception of the viewers. The middle-class, educated producers had constructed for themselves an audience 'in need of enlightenment' and then constructed a product – *Hilmiyya Nights* – to meet that 'need' (1995, pp. 199–200). Both the Cairo domestic servants and the Upper Egyptian peasants very much enjoyed watching the serial but seemed untouched by its political and social messages of self-reliance, political autonomy and anti-consumerism, receiving them as they did within a stream of other messages from American soaps, local chat shows and advertisements for running shoes (1995, pp. 206–7). Abu-Lughod asserts that their experience of television was compartmentalized, lacking any necessary connection to their experience of life, and that *Hilmiyya Nights* was just one item in that compartment. Even the serial's self-professed aim, to introduce the urban working classes and the rural peasantry to a form of high-minded modernity, by returning to them knowledge of their own national history, was too little and came too late. As Abu-Lughod wryly comments, the viewers were already well acquainted with modernity: 'the more common form of modernity in the post-colonial world: the modernity of poverty, consumer desires, underemployment, ill health and religious nationalism' (1995, p. 207).

The main lesson to be taken from Abu-Lughod's study by the social researcher considering an investigation into television is a surprisingly refreshing one: that perhaps television is not quite as socially important as its producers would have us believe. Television – perhaps the most self-absorbed and self-regarding of the mass media – constantly constructs its own viewers, and exercises its agency within a hall of mirrors, shifting its production to meet the needs of these constructed viewers, then commissioning further research to evaluate the success of these shifts upon the constructed objects. Social researchers perhaps need to exercise especial care when entering this charmed circle, to be certain that they have set their own research parameters rather than having uncritically accepted those set up before them. One way out is to take the suggestions of the previous chapter and to pay attention to the materiality of visual culture, in this case the material and social placing of the television set and its output. One consequence of this is to shift analysis away from earlier communication models of television viewership. While the 'reader response' or audience-focused school of analysis that developed in the 1970s and 1980s de-centred the notion of the media producer acting as the only agent (see Morley, 1996, for a good and recent overview; see also Banks, 1996, pp. 118–24), with viewers merely as passive subjects of the producer's action, nonetheless even according viewers agency in interpreting media messages in accordance with their class, gender or ethnic background still rested on a premise of messages being sent, received and interpreted.

One advantage of Abu-Lughod's approach is that because television was not the main focus of her inquiry, she was under no methodological pressure to confirm its importance in daily life. It seems banal, but perhaps necessary, to point out that any sociological investigation that takes television as its prime object of study is almost duty-bound to end up justifying itself by confirming that television is indeed extremely important. Abu-Lughod, unfettered by such an agenda, is free to conclude that *Hilmiyya Nights*, while undoubtedly popular, was hardly a key factor in introducing Egyptian peasants to modernity.

Making television

Although the study of television programming, whether in isolation or in a broader social context, is a mainstay of media studies research, there are surprisingly few empirical studies of television (or film) production. One reason for this might be that few ordinary viewers know very much about the technological and social processes involved and that therefore their 'reading' of television is unaffected by them. Consequently, much social research on television has concentrated on consumption, occasionally treating viewers as passive vessels filled with more or less wholesome messages, but more recently seeing viewers as active subjects engaged in the construction of meaning (but see Morley, 1992, pp. 26-39 for some caveats).

Morley points out that there are indeed connections between production and consumption. His assessment of television as radio-with-pictures is, he claims, shared by television's producers. When first introduced for mass consumption in America in the 1950s, television was intended by its makers as a form of domestic cinema, demanding the viewers' full visual attention. Unfortunately, it was also realized that women, while the primary domestic consumers, would simply not have the time during the housework-filled day to watch in a concentrated fashion and would therefore switch off, missing the crucial advertising breaks.

> The solution which gradually emerged to this problem . . . was the redesign of television programming, not on the model of 'private cinema' requiring close visual attention, but on the model of radio: television as 'radio-with pictures', where the narrative is mainly carried by the soundtrack and the visuals play a subordinate, 'illustrative' role. (Morley, 1995, p. 177)

Busy housewives could now keep the television on constantly while they worked, dropping in and out of the pictures while following the soundtrack. A rise in volume when the advertising break started would catch their attention and bring them back into the room. Mirzoeff (1990) disagrees with this line, beginning with the simple fact that television remote control units always have a mute button to cut the sound, but never a blank button to cut the picture.[22] While a radio-with-pictures model may be appropriate for certain kinds of programming, such as news and current affairs, other kinds such as soap operas and sport demand – and receive – concentrated visual and aural attention (1999, p. 10).

Empirical research is therefore necessary to establish just how television programmes are made and what producers think they are doing, and why. In one of the most exhaustive investigations into how television is made, the media sociologist Roger Silverstone spent the best part of two years with a BBC production team, following the course of a science programme from the initial production meetings through to the eventual screening. Silverstone published his account as an extended diary, though one that while full of detail gives little indication of his research methodology (Silverstone, 1985). The implication is that the study of television production required few if any special skills (though Silverstone had himself once been employed as a BBC researcher and to some extent was familiar with the processes). This is probably entirely correct; there is nothing mysterious about television production and observing the process should pose no more problems than observing social processes of the actors in any organization. Silverstone makes no claims to providing a visual analysis, and there is no obviously visual emphasis in his account. What he does do, however, is to ground production issues sociologically and empirically, such as in his description of how decisions are taken by the producer and editor to use subtitles as opposed to voiceover commentary to translate foreign-language dialogue.

Photo-elicitation

The examples in the previous section concerned research projects that sought to extend the study of television from a mere 'reading' by the researcher (through content analysis, for example) to include research on the producers and consumers. The researchers had little or no control over the images seen by their research subjects, and the process is in that sense rather passive. The researcher can be more active if she selects the images for viewing, and while this can be done with film and television (see below) it is far easier with still photographs.

Photo-elicitation is a straightforward method to understand but rather more difficult to utilize. It involves using photographs to invoke comments, memory and discussion in the course of a semi-structured interview. Specific examples of social relations or cultural form depicted in the photographs can become the basis for a discussion of broader abstractions and generalities; conversely, vague memories can be given sharpness and focus, unleashing a flood of detail. According to John and Malcolm Collier (1986, pp. 105–7), an additional benefit is that the awkwardness that an interviewee may feel from being put on the spot and grilled by the interviewer can be lessened by the presence of photographs to discuss; direct eye contact need not be maintained, but instead interviewee and interviewer can both turn to the photographs as a kind of neutral third party. Awkward

65

silences can be covered as both look at the photographs, and in situations where the status difference between interviewer and interviewee is great (such as between an adult and a child) or where the interviewee feels they are involved in some kind of test, the photographic content always provides something to talk about. But although the basic principles of photo-elicitation rest upon a fairly transparent reading of the internal narrative of photographic content, issues of photographic multivocality and the complexity of the entanglement of photo-graphic objects in human social relations means that photo-elicitation (and the more rarely used film elicitation) is not always so straightforward in practice.

For clarity, we can examine variation in the practice of photo-elicitation by considering the sources and types of photographs used, ranging from examples where the social researcher has little control over the selection of the images – typically those owned by the research subjects already – to those where she plays a more active role up to and including taking the photographs herself with specific research intent (more collaborative ventures are discussed in a later section). In all cases, it would seem that the sociological (as opposed to, say, psychological) value of such projects is strongly reliant on images that are either owned by the subjects of research or very strongly connected to them in some way, such as photographs of their ancestors lodged in a museum or archive. In both these instances, the reasons for the subjects to want to see the photographs and their understanding of the intentions of the interviewer in showing them are relatively straightforward, at least on the surface. More problematic are cases where neither subject nor interviewer has any particularly obvious link to the images, and where the intentions of the researcher may be unclear to the subjects. The most extreme cases of this would perhaps be in certain kinds of laboratory-based psychology experiments, where subjects are shown a sequence of images – photographs of faces, ink blots, Chinese ideograms – and asked to make simple choices without being told what the purpose of the experiment is, or even being deliberately misled, in order to minimize the risk of subjects double-guessing the researcher's preferred outcome.

Photo-elicitation and memory

The use of photo-elicitation in such controlled circumstances is relatively rare in qualitative sociological and anthropological investigations. Indeed, the French anthropologist and psychologist Yannick Geffroy, and the Italian anthropologist Paolo Chiozzi, both describe accidentally stumbling across the technique in the course of fieldwork (Geffroy, 1990; Chiozzi, 1989). In the early 1970s Geffroy and a fellow student at the University of Nice were conducting research on popular traditions surrounding a saint's day festival in a village in the south of France. This involved interviewing elderly members of the village, not just about how the festival had been celebrated decades earlier, but about more general aspects of village life at the time. While fruitful in some ways, both Geffroy and his informants would sometimes find these inquiries about the past frustrating: 'Some descriptions of events could be difficult to express. Often during interviews, we heard these words: 'You should have seen how ...'.' Geffroy describes how the turning point came one day when an elderly woman decided that in fact they could see:

> During her interview ... she stood up suddenly saying 'But ... wait a minute'. . . . She went and opened the doors of an old wall cupboard from which she brought out a large cardboard box, full of photographs, old photographs. ... These family photographs, by helping her memory to recall events and their contexts, allowed us to glean more data and facts from the emotions she was reliving. (1990, p. 374)

In a similar vein, Paolo Chiozzi describes himself as being 'overwhelmed with information' when he first began to use photographs in the course of his interviews (1989, p. 45). In the mid-1980s Chiozzi was conducting research in the Tuscan town of Prato, which had grown four-fold in the previous three decades as a result of migration from elsewhere in Italy. From his account, older inhabitants of the town seemed to be experiencing a sense of 'cultural disintegration' as they sought to come to terms with the recent social and economic changes, but he found specific information and coherent accounts of change hard to come by; not, he thought, as a result of any mistrust on the part of his informants, but simply because of a lack of engagement with him and his project. One day during the course of his research an elderly man told him that his family home in the town's market place had been bombed in the Second World War. By chance, Chiozzi had with him the catalogue of a photographic exhibition that had been held in the town and that depicted the town and the area at the turn of the twentieth century. Looking through the catalogue they quickly identified the house from some general views of the market square. But the elderly informant was not simply seeing his childhood home, a place of personal nostalgic significance, he was seeing a territory – a specific part of the large square that was home to a specific neighbourhood community – and he described the kinship relations between those who lived there, the histories and life courses of particular families in the period leading up to the war in great detail. Chiozzi notes that although he continued his accounts into the post-war period, his recollections became more vague as the town grew and the neighbourhood began to break up: 'It seemed that [he] only then realized how great a transformation had occurred in Prato during his lifetime' (Chiozzi, 1989, pp. 45–6).

Photo-elicitation and ethnicity

Both Chiozzi and Geffroy were largely concerned with social memory in their use of photo-elicitation, and consequently deployed photographs from the periods in which they were interested. But photo-elicitation is equally relevant as a technique with which to investigate contemporary issues. In the course of research with Vietnamese refugees in California, Stephen Gold encountered a range of stereotypes related to an 'internal' ethnic boundary between ethnic Vietnamese and Chinese-Vietnamese, the latter having been an economically powerful but disliked minority in Vietnam (Gold, 1991). Gold cites some previous sociological findings that indicate that self-help strategies resulting in economic co-operation and development within American ethnic groups were a key determinant in the successful adaptation of relatively recently arrived migrants, and was consequently concerned to discover whether the Vietnamese/Chinese-Vietnamese divide was hindering this process amongst the broader community of refugees from Vietnam (1991, p. 9). He made a small selection of his own photographs of both Vietnamese and Chinese-Vietnamese families and individuals in California to conduct photo-elicitation, initially with four key individuals. Each individual – two from each ethnicity, one older and one younger – was shown the photographs in the same order but not confined to a strict interview schedule. All were aware of Gold's broader research frame, and all knew him well. While Gold states that he carefully selected the sample photographs according to certain criteria (variety of social settings, apparent clarity or ambiguity of ethnic markers such as the language of shop signs, and so forth), it does not seem that the photographs were originally taken with the intention of conducting a photo-elicitation exercise.

Gold's first inquiry was in the form of a simple test: could his interviewees correctly identify the ethnicity of the individuals represented merely from a reading of the photographs' manifest content? Setting aside the issue of whether ethnic identification is ever straightforward, no matter how much information is available, Gold notes that while the two older informants guessed 'correctly' with a greater frequency, none of the four was 'correct' in all cases. The exercise nonetheless indicated the variable criteria by which people might make such guesses. While some sought to make judgements based on physiognomy – the shape and size of a photographic subject's nose, for example – others looked to more subtle as well as contextual factors. Images of women in particular were felt to be likely carriers of ethnic clues: for example, the barely noticeable high heels worn by two women in one photograph were said to be clear indicators of Vietnamese ethnicity on the stereotypical grounds that the Vietnamese were more closely associated with the French colonial rulers than the Chinese-Vietnamese; as French people are generally thought to be fashion-conscious, therefore the women must be French-influenced Vietnamese (1991, pp. 13–14). Gold also reports a few findings from his second line of inquiry – to use the photographs to prompt people to discuss the stereotypes each holds of the other and to elaborate upon these. Both sides commented on the greater family orientation of the Chinese-Vietnamese, their willingness to work long and hard, and to utilize kin ties in developing and consolidating business ventures, though one suspects that this kind of information would have been forthcoming anyway, regardless of the use of photographs. Nonetheless, as Gold says and others have confirmed, 'The photos gave respondents an object on which they could focus their discussion of their culture and experiences' (1991, p. 21).

Issues raised by photo-elicitation

These examples present a variety of overall contrasts and lessons, from the limited objective and almost experimental aspect of part of Gold's study to the far more open-ended and phenomenological aspects of Geffroy and Chiozzi's studies. The difference is not, I think, unconnected to the fact that Chiozzi and Geffroy were using old photographs, about which they initially knew little, although there was clearly a strong link between the photographs and the interviewees. Photo-elicitation exercises employing images that are not produced by the researcher, and that do not have any particular link to the subjects in terms of their production or manifest content, seem relatively rare in social research, and probably for good reason. If one of the aims of photo-elicitation is to increase the degree of intimacy between researcher and subject, then arbitrary images, removed from one context and deployed in another, would seem unlikely to promote this. Furthermore, other aspects of the images such as their perceived embedding within another social context may come to dominate the course of the interview, possibly working against the intended research aim.

This appears to have been the case in another anthropological photo-elicitation project, this time located in Indonesia. Wishing to document local textile traditions in Sumatra before they changed beyond recognition, Sandra Niessen was faced with a dilemma: the museum collections she was familiar with in Europe were far too precious to take to the field (even if she had been granted permission to do so), but relying on finding enough examples in Sumatran villages to make a full account was a risk (Niessen, 1991, pp. 416–17). So she took a careful selection of photographs of textiles in museum collections, anticipating that the only difficulty might be that the research subjects might not 'read' the photographs easily (1991, p. 418). This proved not to be the case, but what the subjects 'read' was also the power inequality in the interviewing process; while many were interested in the images and the textiles portrayed, they also expressed a degree of resentment at Niessen's apparent ownership of their objects, an ownership she flaunted by showing them images of the objects (1991, p. 421).

There are strong indications in some of the cases described above that the work of extrapolating from personal memories or experiences prompted by photographs is not solely the task of the researcher alone. Research subjects cannot be treated merely as containers of information that is extracted by the research investigator and then analyzed and assembled elsewhere, and attempts to do so may cause anger or irritation as Niessen found. Rather, the introduction of photographs to interviews and conversations sets off a kind of chain reaction: the photographs effectively exercise agency, causing people to do and think things they had forgotten, or to see things they had always known in a new way, as in the case of Chiozzi's elderly informant who came to a new understanding about the break-up of his neighbourhood community. They serve to bring about a research collaboration between the investigator and subject, an issue that I discuss at greater length below.

Film elicitation

For a variety of reasons, film (and video) are less often used in interview contexts than photographs. One significant difference relates to the materiality of the respective media. While an envelope or album of photographs can be viewed anywhere, in almost any circumstances, even a video cassette of a film will require a player and a power source. In the same vein, photographs can be passed around, picked up and discarded, carried out to the light, or examined with a magnifying glass to get a better or a closer view. The time-based properties of film and video by contrast impose their own constraints upon viewing practice, and researchers need to be aware of these. For example, if specific information is sought relating to the manifest visible content of archival film footage, where the structure within and between scenes is arbitrary or merely chronological, then a researcher might do better to digitize and print off specific frame stills to use in interview contexts.

Eliciting data through film

Nonetheless, there can be value in showing whole films or sequences of film to informants, and this is well exemplified in Stephanie Krebs's work on the Thai dance-drama known as Khon (Krebs, 1975). Her research took place in the early 1970s, well before videotape was available to the amateur, yet the nature of the inquiry demanded moving rather than still images. Krebs had hypothesized that gestures used in the dance communicated meaning, and represented key or core Thai cultural values that were distilled within the dance-drama. She systematically shot sequences of the dance, first using Super-8 film and later using 16 mm film and cameras, to provide material for a set of interlinked elicitation exercises. The Super-8 material was shown, unsatisfactorily, to informants using a modified projector, and the 16 mm material was shown on a small or baby Steenbeck editing table. It must be said that Krebs's view of film is unabashedly realist, at least for herself if not her informants: '[film is a] "slice of reality" ... the informant MUST accept at least part of the screened event as reality ... ' (1975, pp. 283–4, emphasis in original). This positivist and realist approach allowed her to set up and control experimental parameters – for example, showing the same sequence of film to a number of informants and asking them the same questions, as free of prompts and cues as possible, or screening a section without sound to determine whether dance gestures communicated unambiguously or only in the context of the accompanying song.

Although she largely shot and edited her own film material, Krebs was essentially working with raw footage and asking her informants to concentrate entirely upon manifest content (or at least she seems to have assumed that this is what they were doing). She assumes that in most societies a realist reading is normative and unproblematic, and that even in societies unfamiliar with moving pictures it would be relatively straightforward to 'introduce' the members to this form of representation and then begin elicitation. While this may be true in a purely perceptual sense – the translation between a perception of three-dimensional reality in the round, and a two-dimensional representation of it – what images of one's own society, or those of another, mean when one is required to look at them is dependent on the broader frame of context. Abu-Lughod's Egyptian peasants saw the didactic images of *Hilmiyya Nights* against a background of American soap operas and images of consumerism; Niessen's Batak villagers saw the 'neutral' images of textile designs against a background of colonialism and exploitation.

Eliciting opinions through film

A more exploratory approach to film elicitation was taken by the anthropological filmmaking team of Tim Asch, Patsy Asch and Linda Connor in their filmic and anthropological exploration of the life and work of Jero Tapakan, a Balinese masseuse and spirit medium. The team collaborated to produce a film of Jero, *A Balinese Trance Séance* (1980), which shows her at work as a medium, meeting clients on the veranda of her village home and going into trance to allow the deities and other spirits to speak through her to the clients.

After the film was completed, the team returned to Bali and screened it (on video, in a house in a nearby town) for Jero, taking note of her reactions and filming the proceedings (resulting in *Jero on Jero: A Balinese Trance Séance Observed,* 1980). Far from being absorbed with her on-screen representation, Asch and Connor (1994) note that Jero glanced at it occasionally but seemed more interested in engaging Connor in conversation. Connor, in contrast, fixed her gaze resolutely on the screen, often talking to Jero without looking at her. They go on:

> Linda knows the film will only last 30 minutes and that we have very limited footage to record Jero's reactions. There are many topics she wants to cover in that time. Linda directs her gaze primarily at the TV and

71

indicates she wants Jero to look at specific bits and to respond to certain questions. But Jero ignores many of Linda's gestural and facial clues.
She has never seen the film before, doesn't know how long it will last,
and is not used to working within specified time periods. (1994, p. 17)

Asch and Connor go on to point out that the film viewing does indeed elicit
further information concerning spirit mediumship, though they also point out that
Jero quickly arrives at her own agenda. Knowing that the viewing session is being
filmed and will therefore be seen by others, she takes the opportunity to correct
any (mistaken) impression viewers may take away from the earlier film that it is
she who is providing advice and help for her clients. Instead she modestly defers
to the power of the deities and spirits, for whom she is merely a channel.

Jero's attempt to control the elicitation session is in keeping with Paul ten
Have's comment on ethnomethodological uses of film (or video) elicitation. If
people are shown a video recording of their own actions and asked to comment
on it (on the grounds that they know best why they did something), their
responses will be framed by the context of the interview itself, rather than that of
the original actions (ten Have, 2004, p. 72). More generally, while photo- and
film elicitation (or today, video elicitation) are much used in many kinds of social
research, it is a mistake to limit the use of the technique to that of eliciting data
about image content. As well as the internal narrative of the image – the story it
is telling to the viewer – there are two external narratives to consider: there is not
only the immediate here-and-now context of the interview itself, there is also the
there-then context of the image's original production. Research subjects may or
may not know the details of the production context, but they will undoubtedly
infer it.

Making pictures

In Krebs's work on the Thai dance-drama, images were created by the social
researcher specifically for the purpose of subsequent film elicitation; in the case
of the Asch, Asch and Connor team we can suppose that the first film was made
for its own sake but the idea of using it for film-elicitation purposes subsequently
presented itself. Many images created by social researchers are not of this kind,
however. Instead, a variety of other analytical agendas lie behind the image-
creation process, sometimes reflexively considered by the researcher, sometimes
not. In this section I look at the justifications and practicalities of image-making
by the social researcher.

There is not the space in this section, nor do I necessarily have the competence, to discuss the technicalities of taking still and moving images in the field;
there are several guides available.[23] In terms of general tips the most basic is probably 'get to know your equipment' combined with 'practice, practice, practice';

conducting social research in the field is quite stressful enough without having to worry about which button to press. The second tip, following on from the first, is to avoid or ignore all features on a camera (video or digital stills) that alter the image electronically while in the camera (non-optical zoom, captioning, cropping, etc.); all such modifications, if desired, can be performed later manually or by software, and for the same reason all digital images should be shot at the highest possible resolution. 'Features' should always take second place to the quality of the basic components and overall robustness when selecting a camera of any kind for field use. The final tip is take copious notes: at the very least, day, time, persons present, and so forth should be noted, as one would with field notes or audio recordings. Some, such as Victor Caldarola (see below) advocate much more extensive notes, reflexively examining one's intentions and motivations in creating the image, as well as technical data concerning lighting levels, film stock, and so on.

Documentation

Bearing in mind the analytical approaches discussed in the last chapter that develop Foucault's concepts of the panopticon and surveillance, it should be obvious that the aim of mere documentation can never be a neutral enterprise. It is worthwhile making a distinction between use and intention at this point. Plenty of people, not just social researchers, create visual images for the purpose of 'mere' documentation. Estate agents, for example, take photographs to illustrate the printed details of property they wish to sell, museum curators take photographs of the objects in their collections to illustrate catalogues, plastic surgeons take photographs against measuring charts to show the profile of noses destined for change. The *use* of photography in these and many other instances is clearly a social act (what persuades people to buy houses? why do people have nose jobs?) and amenable to social analysis, but the *intention* on the part of the photographer at the point of image creation is largely or wholly documentary, whatever her underlying and perhaps unconscious motivation. So, too, a social researcher can have purely documentary intentions when creating images, and while these intentions may be subject to the scrutiny of later social researchers, this does not invalidate the original intentionality.

That is not to say image-making in a documentary mode is a straightforward matter. Many anthropologists and others use still or moving image technologies to document material processes – basket weaving, cloth dyeing, and so on. Sometimes these exercises, perhaps inadvertently, become exercises in exploration and discovery rather than simple documentation. For example, John Collier took a series of photographs to document the weaving of raw wool into finished textile by Otavalo Indians in Ecuador in the 1940s (Collier and Collier, 1986, pp. 71–4). After he had photographed the first stages of the process (washing, drying and carding of the wool), he developed the film, printed contacts and showed the results to the weaver. The weaver was not pleased and considered that the photographs had shown him to be a poor weaver. He insisted that Collier re-photographed the same stages, while he indicated when and precisely what Collier should photograph.

Such instances can lead to a heightened reflexivity on the part of the social researcher, requiring her to ask the same questions concerning the internal and external narrative of the images she produces as she would of the internal and external narratives of images she encountered: what do I intend this to be a picture of? why am I taking it now? what am I excluding from the frame? and so on. More than one social researcher has highlighted the need to be aware of and to overcome unconscious or taken-for-granted approaches towards the use of still photography, even in 'mere' documentation. Victor Caldarola, an experienced photographer accompanying his anthropologist wife on a research trip to South Kalimantan, Indonesia, consciously adopted three guiding premises that made his own understanding explicit (Caldarola, 1985). First, that photographic images are event-specific representations (a denial, at least in the documentary research context, of a photographic representation to make generalizing claims); second, that any meaning in the image is dependent upon the context in which it was produced (not merely the narrative or content it portrays); and third, that the production of photographic images is a social event, involving communication and mutual understanding on the part of both image-maker and image-subject.

The consequences of this approach are multiple, including not least the assumption that any images shown to a third party without any other information are considered meaningless. Caldarola's methodology was to take copious notes as he photographed the duck rearing and egg production that formed the chief sector of the local economy. In these notes he describes not only what he thinks is taking place before the camera, but also indications of his own intentions in taking the images, and the circumstances – social and technical – of their production. Caldarola's methodology was also iterative: he took photographs, interviewed subjects with the photographs, took more photographs in response to their comments, and so on.

This iterative process lies at the heart of so-called grounded theory, briefly mentioned in the last chapter, where data are gathered in stages, analyzed, and used to assess the initial hypothesis or research question, in a spiralling process until a point is reached where further data add no further insight. In yet another photo-elicitation study, a Swiss anthropologist, Ricabeth Steiger, adopted grounded theory to guide her study, reformulating her theoretical stance as the research revealed new findings (Steiger, 1995, p. 29; Glaser and Strauss, 1967). In this research, designed to explore the change in family dynamics of Swiss professional couples upon the arrival of their first child, she took her own photographs specifically for the study, and describes in some detail the technical issues she had to consider.

This included the fact that her theoretical orientation and working hypotheses were liable to change during the course of the research in response to what her subjects said or did, and thus the criteria for composition, lighting, and so forth could never be fixed or absolute. Her basic methodology was to conduct an initial semi-structured interview with subjects, take a series of photographs, and then return for a follow-up photo-elicitation session (1995, pp. 29–30). As she was concerned primarily with mothers, many of Steiger's images were of mothers in their home environments, as well as views of that environment as seen by the mothers (such as the view from their kitchen windows). But as the focus was also on the mothers' relationship with their children, several images were taken from a child's point of view – low down, at child's eye-level. Although the underlying approach was exploratory, Steiger was in some sense allowing her camera to 'document' the changing phases of her analytical understandings.

Making movies

A film or video camera can of course also be used in the ways described above and often is, for example in documenting material culture processes or dance performances. And of course 'documentary' is a generic term for non-fiction film, as well as being associated with a specific form of non-fiction film (see Chapter 1). But while the power of the moving image camera to represent rather than merely document is no greater than that of the stills camera, it is often treated as though it were, because the properties of time and movement that the film or video camera seeks to capture, combined with the time-based viewing experience, reproduce familiar forms of narrative to Euro-American viewers. While, especially in the early days, ethnographic films sought to 'show' (that is, document) rather than 'tell' (see Grimshaw, 2001, p. 19), the fact that film could tell a story was quickly seized upon and exploited. Once codes for editing had begun to develop, to exploit the narrative potential still further, it became almost inevitable that social researchers using first film and then video cameras would seek not only to document their research, or to gather moving-image data, but to make movies.

Making a film, as opposed to simply shooting footage, involves editing and other post-production tasks, such as adding subtitles, but it also rests upon a series of ideas concerning the place of visual representation within social science itself. Within anthropology, the discipline most closely associated with film production, there is an ongoing debate over whether an ethnographic film can be a free-standing product of social research inquiry or whether it needs to be complemented by other outputs, such as a written ethnography or a study guide. The issue is not so much one of representation, but of epistemology. If there are ways of knowing the social world that are independent of language, then some would argue that creating a film is a suitable way to explore and represent that knowledge. Grimshaw, for example, states that anthropological filmmaking requires 'a fundamental re-orientation of [the anthropological] perspective such that the world is not primarily approached through language, explanation or generalization, but through a re-embodiment of the self as the foundation for renewed engagement with everyday life' (cited in Henley, 2004, p. 111). While agreeing that film can represent the embodied experience of social life in a way that words cannot, Henley does not wish to abandon a language-based approach to social life altogether and argues instead for an accommodation between filmmaking and text-making (Henley, 2004, pp. 111–12). Heider, representing an older and more positivist approach in the discipline, simply states that written study guides are a necessary adjunct to ethnographic film: to put all the 'information' required for anthropological analysis into the film itself (in the form of a verbal commentary) would turn it into little more than an illustrated lecture (Heider, 1976, p. 127 and *passim*).

Clearly this is not a methodological issue, but there are methodological consequences. If a researcher takes Heider's line, for example, then the way in which she operates the camera in the field will be very different from the way Grimshaw might use it. The French anthropologist and filmmaker Jean Rouch is famous for describing what he called 'ciné-trance', an immersion by the film-maker into the process of filming that goes so deep that the filmmaker and camera become fused (Rouch, 1975, p. 94).[24] Rouch also used fictionalized scenes in his films and both this and the ciné trance require stances towards the image and filmic practices in the field that differ markedly from those adopted when making a film that documents the building of a house, for example, or throwing a pot. While Rouch was working (in the 1960s and 1970s) to an agenda that was very much his own rather than that dictated by the anthropological theory of his time, others have responded more directly to changing ideas in the discipline. Lutkehaus and Cool (1999) describe a number of films, many inspired by Rouch's early work, produced by students and others at the Center for Visual Anthropology at the University of Southern California that have responded to the so-called crisis in representation in anthropology, discussed in the previous chapter.

Other films, such as Barbash and Taylor's *In and Out of Africa* (1992), respond to recent calls within anthropology (e.g. Marcus, 1995; Gupta and Ferguson, 1992) for the discipline to 'deterritorialize', that is, to dispense with the assumption that a people or a community are defined by where they live. In an increasingly transnational world some groups of people form communities that span the globe, and even for those people who are born and die in the same village their lives are touched by global influences. Barbash and Taylor go a step beyond this, filming not so much people on the move, but objects on the move – in this case West African wood carvings, which we see with their producers, traders and consumers in Africa and New York.

Analysis within the film text   Films such as *In and Out of Africa* could be said to respond to shifts in theory and analysis. Some filmmakers, again within an anthropological tradition, have sought to go a step further and encode theoretical or analytical insights within the film itself. Peter Biella (1988) and Don Rundstrom (1988) both claim to have inserted anthropological analysis directly into the internal narrative of their films in quite formalist ways, through consciously adopting particular camera angles and editing styles. Rundstrom's film *The Path* (1971), for example, is a highly constructed film about the Japanese tea ceremony, which uses colour, camera angle and frame to convey a Japanese aesthetic sensibility rather than a realist representation. Ruby advocates what he calls 'trompe l'oeil' realism, a strategy that exploits documentary film's potential to present an apparently realist view of the world and then to subvert it by reflexively drawing attention to the film's own creation. In this way audiences are forced to confront the (inherently analytical) construction of knowledge that the internal narrative conveys (Ruby, 2000, chaps 6 and 10). The reflexivity that Ruby advocates has been seen elsewhere, however; indeed, few documentaries of any sort today adhere to the old 'voice of God' mode in which a disembodied and socially unlocatable filmmaker/narrator omnisciently comments on the images, or imputes thoughts and feelings to the films' subjects (Nichols, 1988).

A step beyond the filmmaker revealing her motivations in creating the film, and revealing her presence as part of the action, lies in having the film subjects themselves provide the broader context of their lives and the filming process. A typical technique is to ask a research subject being filmed to 'show us around' – to describe the immediate physical environment. In a sequence at the start of *To Live with Herds* (1972), an ethnographic film about East African pastoralists, David MacDougall asks the main character to 'describe the extent of Jie territory', which he does by pointing out features on the horizon and naming the various other pastoralist groups who live in this arid area of Uganda; similarly, in the MacDougalls' *Lorang's Way* (1977), Lorang, a Kenyan Turkana elder, shows the filmmakers around his compound, explaining features as he goes along. The same technique is adopted by John Baily when he asks Amir, a refugee Afghani musician in Pakistan, to show him around the single-room house he shares with his wife, parents-in-law and children (in *Amir*, 1985). In all these cases, what is elicited is not merely a catalogue of physical features, but a narrative that uses those buildings and objects as containers for biographical and social knowledge: Amir's itemization of his possessions allows him to reflect on his refugee experience, for example. Asking research subjects and film participants to reflect on their own lives, not in an isolated interview context but within their physical and social environment, would seem to allow a greater possibility for the kind of embodied and experiential analytical perspectives called for by Grimshaw.

Collaborative projects

Case study: Photographic voices – the potential for action research

The case study presented at the beginning of Chapter 1 described two studies where children were given cameras as a way of allowing researchers to see parts of their lives that might not otherwise be visible, such as their places of employment. 'Action research' in educational studies aims to go a step beyond this and provide insights into how school environments might be changed. Although not conceived of as a piece of action research, Michael Schratz and Ulrike Steiner-Löffler (1998) clearly saw the potential in giving cameras to primary school children as a way of generating insight. Schratz and Steiner-Löffler are concerned that the opinions of children, and particularly very young children, are usually ignored when it comes to school self-evaluation, the reasoning being that they lack the written and linguistic dexterity required to complete complex forms or write elaborate reports.

Having successfully used cameras with older children, they decided to attempt it with primary school children (in Vienna). Presumably in order to simplify the task, the children were asked to take photographs that addressed a simple question: 'Where in school do you feel good, where not and why not?' Schratz and Steiner-Löffler's methodology is best summarized by the 'short guide to photo-evaluation' they give in their article:

- teams are formed from four to five self-selected pupils, one of whom will act as photographer;
- each team discusses 'good' and 'bad' places and how they should be photographed (for example, should people be in the shot or not);
- the teams take the photographs;
- once developed, the photographs are presented on a poster together with reasons for their selection and the posters presented to the class.

By way of results from this project, places such as the playground were selected as 'good' places, and the craftroom as a bad place (because they did not like the teacher). There were, however, some ambiguous places, such as the staff room and the toilets (which Schratz and Steiner-Löffler view as 'taboo' places) and also disagreements, the exploration of which led to further insight into the children's perception of their own environment.

In this particular case, Schratz and Steiner-Löffler did not in fact go on to the next stage of the project, which would have been for the teams to then discuss how to get changes made in their environment, but they clearly flag its potential.

If watching television with research subjects is a relatively passive 'method' for the social researcher, it is at least an activity with which the research subjects are engaged and that is familiar to them. The same cannot be said of some other visual methods, such as photo-elicitation or video documentation, which research subjects may not understand or find pointlessly time-consuming. As Niessen says, 'I do not think that generally an interview is an exciting occasion for a Batak' (1991, p. 421). At worst, research subjects may be hostile to the real or imagined purpose of the process. Of course, this is true for any field-based social research, not just visual research, but there are special considerations when using a stills or video camera as part of the research process. For some people in some contexts being filmed or photographed can be associated with danger, control and surveillance; for example, when police or security agents film crowds of protesters, their intentions may be as much to intimidate as to document.

Setting aside the ethical dimension for a moment (discussed below), one practical solution to the problem is to devise a research agenda that is collaborative, one that involves the interests and concerns of both the researcher and the research subjects. All field-based social research involves collaboration at some level, but as often as not the research subjects agree to become involved in the research out of politeness, or because they cannot think of a good way of saying no, or perhaps even because they are paid. Even if they understand the point of the research (indeed, even if they understand the concept of 'research' in the first place), and even if they think its aims are laudable and worth supporting, the focus of the research is not necessarily the most important thing in their lives. They may co-operate (rather than collaborate) in the hope of satisfying personal agendas,[25] or because they are bored or lonely. At the same time, they may have other concerns on their minds – poor housing, sick children, land claims. These and many other issues are all fruitful topics for social research, are areas where researcher and research subjects can collaborate, and are rich in potential for visual methodologies. Some more explicitly collaborative and political projects are discussed below. First, I briefly consider a number of cases of more inadvertent collaboration.

Collaboration in photo-elicitation

Sometimes a social researcher with a camera but no particular visual agenda decides to take some photographs of her research subjects for reasons not directly related to the research; this might be to show friends and family back at home, or in the hope that by taking their photos and giving them copies the researcher will become closer to her research subjects. Although not quite in this category (she is a visual anthropologist), Pink describes how even this apparently simple task can become a methodology. Asked by her neighbours in Guinea Bissau to take their photographs, Pink would go to their houses in the morning when she judged the light to be best, only to be turned away by busy women who were wearing torn work clothes and who had not attended to their hair. Later, when they were ready and had attired themselves in the way they wished to be seen, they would come to her for the photograph. As Pink notes, rather than seeing this as a failure (from her point of view), the experience could be turned to advantage as a methodology, giving her valuable insights into self-representation (2001, pp. 59–60).

An attempt to control one's visual representation has already been mentioned above, with the case of the Ecuadorian weaver who demanded that John Collier retake a sequence of material process images, considering that the originals showed him to be a poor weaver. Elsewhere, research subjects have attempted to influence a researcher's image-making practices in other ways. Chiozzi, mentioned above in connection with an 'accidental' photo-elicitation project in Tuscany, found that another group of research subjects again reacted positively to being shown old photographs of their region (rural northern Tuscany), but they also insisted that Chiozzi re-photograph the same sites in an attempt to make manifest what they saw as the loss of their cultural identity (Chiozzi, 1989, p. 46). Although Chiozzi does not dwell on this point, it would seem that although in one sense the changes in the landscape and habitat patterns of the valley were perfectly visible to the original inhabitants' eyes, their insistence that a photographic record be made was a way of concretizing this, of externalizing in material form something that until then had been tacit, internal and subjective.

Moving beyond this to a greater sense of collaboration, there is the case of a group of research students at the University of Amsterdam who decided to employ this methodology from the beginning. In a study of ethnic integration in a run-down neighbourhood of The Hague, the students chose to have their research subjects dictate the subject of the images, rather than relying on pre-existing images or deciding for themselves what images to take. Each student asked a research subject to take him or her on a tour of the neighbourhood and asked the subject to point out what (visual) aspects of the environment they wished to comment upon; nothing, including 'ethnic integration', was specifically suggested as a topic. The subjects were then interviewed about the images and asked to suggest other photographs that could be taken and again interviewed subsequently. Finally, the subjects (who did not know one another) were shown each others' images and asked to comment (van der Does et al., 1992). This proved to be revealing; although none of the subjects apparently chose to have images of the neighbourhood's ethnic diversity created, some commented on it in subsequent interviews.

One image, of a number of white Dutch women and their children sitting on a bench, and a group of Moroccan and Turkish women and their children sitting on an adjacent bench, was claimed by one research subject to 'show' a lack of ethnic integration (presumably because of the bench segregation) while another claimed it 'showed' the opposite (presumably because all the women and children were using the same public play area) (1992, p. 56). Additionally, some subjects directed the students to take images of the same thing, but from different angles. Two chose a rather brutal sculpture of a horse in a local park, for example, but one wanted to have it shown from the front to give a pleasant impression of the park, while another wanted it shown from the rear, to show how unpleasant the park could be (1992, pp. 22, 30, 52). In both cases the research subjects were seeking to say something in their choice of images, both to the researchers and to anyone who might subsequently come across the image. That what they wanted to say appears contrary is an indication that 'communities' do not necessarily speak with one voice, whether literally or visually, but one could also interpret their choices as being two sides of the same coin: both felt that a token piece of public art was not really a solution to deep-rooted social problems, but one used the image to indicate potential, what could be done, while the other chose to use the image to indicate what was, how life was actually experienced in the neighbourhood.

Finally, there are several cases where social researchers have given cameras to the research subjects and asked them to create their own images. Two are briefly described in the case study in Chapter 1 ('Seeing through the eyes of children'). The idea here is that such research subject-generated images can either reveal the subjects' own understandings of photography, and perhaps of representation more generally (Sharples et al., 2003), or aspects of the research subjects' lives and environments that are simply unavailable to the researcher (Mizen, 2005). For visual anthropologists the best-known project of this type is Worth and Adair's attempt to extend the Whorf–Sapir hypothesis concerning language and cognition into the realm of the visual, which involved giving film cameras to cinematographically illiterate Navajo people and telling them to film what they liked (Worth and Adair, 1972).[26]

All these examples, except perhaps the last, are essentially variations on the photo-elicitation method but extended to include a heightened degree of collaboration on the part of the research subjects, although in each case described, the initial project was initiated by the social researcher rather than by the research subjects themselves. The experience of those who have tried it – or subsequently commented on the process – would seem to suggest that the final methodology of handing over the camera completely can be problematic, especially if the researcher is not present when the images are taken. This is largely for analytical and intellectual reasons; for one thing, the work is intended, after all, as a piece of social research and all the stages need to be documented, while for another, if the researcher deliberately steps back from the image-making process, the project becomes less collaborative, with the research subject performing 'a task' the results of which are subsequently analyzed, perhaps without any further input from the research subject.

This latter course of action is fine if that is what was intended, but perhaps does not fit so well with a stated aim of collaborative research. Another, more pragmatic reason for the researcher maintaining control over the equipment, relates to the ease of use. While many, but not all, Euro-Americans can probably operate an automatic stills camera easily enough and would require little if any training, things are considerably more complicated when video and especially 16 mm film cameras are used, especially when it comes to editing. Not only is a fair degree of practice necessary, if not training, but the research subjects may end up concentrating far more on 'getting it right' technically than on the image(s) they are seeking to create. While the study of this in itself would be – and is – a legitimate area of social research (for example, the whole field of human/computer interaction [HCI] is devoted to this), not only is research in this area beyond the scope of this book, it is also something that the researcher should be sure that she wants to study, and not a side-track that she fails to recognize. On the other hand, too much control may close off perfectly relevant areas of inquiry, as well as fail to build the goodwill that collaborative ventures depend upon: the Pink and Chiozzi cases above are good examples of responding to unanticipated turns that arise in the course of field research. The strategy adopted by the Dutch research students seems particularly worthy of emulation: control over the structure of the research is set and retained by the researcher(s), but research subjects are encouraged to provide the content.

Collaborative movies

If the projects described above are cases of 'inadvertent' collaboration, or if the impetus to collaboration has come from the social researcher rather than the research subjects, what would research subject-led collaboration look like? In some ways it is hard to imagine how this would occur; in many cases, such as those of children or people living far from metropolitan centres, their knowledge of and access to social researchers is limited or non-existent. It is generally only the rich, the powerful or the well connected who commission research on themselves (but see below on politicized indigenous groups). There are exceptions, however, mostly connected to ongoing anthropological research projects where at some point the research subjects ask the anthropologist to help them make a film, or mount a photographic exhibition.

There are also cases where research subjects ask for help in a matter during the course of which a particular visual methodology presents itself as appropriate. In the course of a research project on social networks in a poor neighbourhood of Lisbon, Ruud van Wezel was asked by his research subjects to help them in their attempts to obtain legal housing. Although the research subjects were poorly educated, the *fotonovella* (a fictional strip-cartoon using photographs, speech bubbles and captions to tell a story) was a popular form of entertainment. At their instigation van Wezel took a series of photographs and created a *fotonovella* about house-building that distilled their concerns, their knowledge and van Wezel's research. The *fotonovella* was then printed cheaply and sold locally (van Wezel, 1988). In another case, anthropologist Howard Morphy and linguist Frances Morphy were conducting research with an Aboriginal community in northern Australia when they were asked to help the group in a land rights case. In the absence of written titles to land, Morphy and Morphy were able to use archival photographs of the area, taken by early missionaries, to elicit information about land use and ownership from elderly members of the group. As well as supplying valuable oral testimony that could be used in the land claim case, Morphy and Morphy also gained access to information that they might not otherwise have had (Howard Morphy, personal communication).

Film and political action

Such use of professional researchers and their visual technologies is increasingly common among politicized groups, such as indigenous peoples in North America and Australia. Strictly speaking, these could not all necessarily be categorized as collaborative research projects; in many cases the researcher is performing as an advocate or facilitator for the group rather than trying to pursue an intellectual agenda deriving from their social science discipline.[27] Some methodological and analytical issues can nonetheless be derived from such projects. For example, as with van Wezel's Portuguese experience above, finding an appropriate visual form is of paramount importance. Vincent Carelli, a Brazilian indigenous rights activist, has been involved with indigenous community video projects for over twenty years (Aufderheide, 1995; see also Carelli, 1988). Although video might seem an inappropriate visual medium for forest-dwelling Amerindians, Carelli recounts the experience of one group's leader who 'instantly grasped the possibilities' of community activist video when it was explained to him, his visual frame of reference being Hollywood action films (presumably viewed in the nearby town) of which he was a great fan (cited in Aufderheide, 1995, p. 86).

In another case, Tim Quinlan had been conducting research with animal herders in Lesotho, southern Africa, and discussed with them the possibility of making a film with them to show the potentially damaging effects that a new conservation management policy might have on their livelihoods. Although some of the older men were familiar with the medium of film, having seen technical training films and feature films during periods of labour migrancy in South Africa, most were not. Quinlan and his team therefore made up a short demonstration video, consisting of scenes of themselves travelling, interviews and episodes from earlier field trips, which then acted as a successful focal point for discussion and explanation (Criticos and Quinlan, 1991, pp. 47–8).

Case study: Kayapó video

One of the best documented cases of indigenous video production in collaboration with an anthropologist, and serving the aims of both, is the Kayapó video project. Anthropologist Terence Turner has been working with the Kayapó, a large
Brazilian Amerindian group, continually since the 1960s. In the 1980s Turner facilitated access for several television crews to come and film the Kayapó, who
were at the time becoming increasingly politicized, particularly over the threat
of a planned dam project that would flood part of their lands. Well used to
dealing with outsiders, the Kayapó quickly saw the potential that film, video
and mass media could have to publicize their cause, and as a result Turner
helped them to obtain first video recording equipment and then editing equipment (Turner, 1990, 1992). The Kayapó initially used the medium as originally
intended – to document their encounters with the Brazilian state, a form of
visual evidence. They also used video for 'internal' purposes, to document
dances and rituals that could be studied by younger people.

But Turner in his continued studies of their video use also noted other aspects,
which feed directly into contemporary anthropological concerns. For example,
while 'documenting' their encounters with agents of the state over the proposed dam, the Kayapó were also aware of the power of the visually arresting
contrast between a forest-dwelling Indian, attired in paint and feathers, and
the sleek and sophisticated video cameras they were using (1992, p. 7). Trading
upon metropolitan stereotypes, the Kayapó camera-operators presented an
image of 'Stone Age' man wielding late-twentieth-century technology that
proved attractive to Brazilian and international journalists who were covering
the dispute. In pursuit of their land rights the Kayapó became adept at manip-
ulating their self-representation.

Examples such as the collaboration between Quinlan and the Lesotho herders are
sometimes hailed as empowering projects, whereby visual media aid disempowered
people in gaining greater control of their lives (see, for example, the somewhat tri-
umphalist tone of the opening scenes to an otherwise very informative film about
Inuit broadcasting in Canada called *Starting Fire with Gunpowder*: Poisy and
Hanson, 1991). There are many critics of this position, from the gentle (e.g. Ginsburg,
1991) to the severe (e.g. Faris, 1992, 1993), and it is indeed naïve to assume that video
or still photography alone can overcome social injustice at a stroke.

However it is clear that in some cases, such as that of the Kayapó (see case
study), disempowered people can co-opt or appropriate visual media, alongside a
range of other strategies aimed at gaining autonomy or rights, or merely to try and
preserve a way of life threatened by global forces, as in the case of the Inuit
and central Australian Aboriginal groups, both of whom have sought to limit
what they see as the culturally destructive effects of dominant (white) television
broadcasting by setting up their own broadcasting stations (Dowmunt, 1993;

Michaels, 1986, 1991a, 1991b). From a purely academic point of view, studies of such appropriations can generate insights into processes of social and cultural change and the tension between globalizing forces and local-level reworkings of identity. Methodologically, then, social researchers should be alert to the possibility of collaborating with research subjects in visual projects, be they modest (Pink's photographs of her neighbours in Guinea Bissau) or large-scale (Michaels helping to establish Aboriginal satellite broadcasting).

Intellectual justifications for collaboration

While some might regard the moral and ethical dimension as sufficient justification for initiating collaborative projects with research subjects, others might not (for example, funding bodies with a strictly academic agenda), in which case it is worth summarizing the intellectual justification. Interpretive analysis in the social sciences (see Box 2.1 in Chapter 2) rests on the notion that 'data' do not exist autonomously and prior to the conduct of research, but are rather produced by the researcher and research subject at the moment(s) of their encounter. In this sense, then, all research projects – visual or otherwise – are collaborative, but if the research subject's role in constructing 'data' through the process of encounter is overlooked, there is a strong danger that the analyst will misinterpret the findings. (A simple example of this would be a research subject giving an untruthful response to a questionnaire question because that is what she thought the researcher wished to hear.) Consequently, in order to ensure that a researcher has the best access to the thoughts, words and deeds of the research subjects, bringing those subjects' opinions on the research itself into the research process would seem not only to be justified but methodologically indispensable.

Sarah Pink takes the idea of collaboration a step further in her advocacy of what she terms 'applied visual anthropology'. By this, she means 'the use of the visual as a tool of social intervention' (2006, p. 82) and she discusses a number of examples in which anthropologists have used film or photography to enhance educational, health or social welfare projects (Pink, 2006, chap. 5). Such work is inherently collaborative, not least because in many cases it is communities or organizations that initiate the project (rather than the researcher) and it is they who form the primary group of 'users' (rather than the researcher's academic peers). As the focus of the present volume is to aid the researcher who is planning to execute her own research, I shall say little more about such applied, user-initiated research. But I would commend Pink's discussion – which is by no means limited to anthropology – to visual researchers who are considering a career beyond the academy.

Ethics

I have already touched on the issue of ethics a number of times and it is now appropriate to embark on a full discussion. Ethical considerations are relevant to all stages of a social research project from its initial conception to the final dissemination of results and beyond, and consequently I could have woven a discussion of ethics throughout the whole of this book. Instead it seems logical to group the discussions in a single section for ease of reference, but in doing so I certainly do not wish to suggest that ethical considerations can or should be bracketed off in any way, a necessary but tiresome component that can be dealt with (on a grant application form for example) and then set aside. As noted in Chapter 1, visual research methodologies would be combined with a variety of other research methodologies in the course of a normal social research project and consequently ethical consideration must be given to all aspects of the research process. As well as the specific considerations discussed in the other books in this *Kit* with regard to interviewing, observation and so on, there are now a number of publications discussing social research ethics in general (e.g. Israel and Hay, 2006; de Laine, 2000) and in fieldwork-based anthropology (e.g. Meskell and Pels, 2005), as well as some more specifically oriented towards visual research (e.g. Pink, 2001; Prosser, 2000). In addition, several disciplinary bodies have established their own ethical guidelines – for example, that produced by my own professional body, the UK and Commonwealth Association of Social Anthropologists.[28] These all provide valuable bases for building an ethical framework around the proposed project as a whole, but are there any specific considerations that the use and creation of visual materials entail?

Ethics and anonymity

The most obvious point of distinctiveness concerns anonymity, or rather, the inability to maintain anonymity given the indexical nature of photomechanical representations. In general, all social researchers agree that unless there is a strong justification for doing otherwise, the social researcher has a duty to protect the privacy of research subjects. Thus, both covert research (where the subjects of research do not realize that research is being conducted) and the publication or dissemination of details that might identify unique individuals are generally frowned upon. In some forms of social research, such as that employing large-scale surveys, the issue rarely arises as data from individuals are quickly ameliorated into clusters and categories and presented in numerical form. In other forms of research that draw upon life or case histories, anonymity and privacy can be assured by the use of pseudonyms for people and places when publishing the results.[29] Generally, this is not possible when it comes to visual research. This is immediately obvious in cases where the researcher creates still or moving images of research subjects, but it also applies to research conducted on pre-existing images.

In the article on visual content analysis that I cite in Chapter 3, Philip Bell reproduces 40 cover images from an Australian woman's magazine (P. Bell,

2001, pp 11–12). The images are hardly larger than postage stamps, but each features a head and shoulders or three-quarter-length shot of a woman, each of whom is presumably still recognizable to herself or those who know her. There is no indication in the article or elsewhere in the edited volume that these women's permission was sought to (re)use their images in this way. This is not surprising: the women are presumably all professional models and at the time of the original photo-shoot they or their agents would have signed contracts agreeing what use could be made of the images. Furthermore, at the time of publication each woman's image would have been seen by tens, perhaps hundreds of thousands of people across Australia and beyond, and to that extent these are in part 'public' images. Bell's treatment of the images is largely neutral; he does not comment on any particular image, let alone any particular woman depicted, and the point of his analysis is not to say anything about the women themselves but to suggest ways in which content analysis can indicate shifts in the magazine's self-image over a quarter of a century.

The point of this discussion is not to suggest any kind of ethical breach on Bell's part – far from it; this seems an entirely reasonable use of the images that neither intends nor implies any harm to the women. So what would have to alter for a use of images like these to become problematic? The author might (subjectively) claim that some of the older cover models were 'ugly' and in the later period sampled the magazine had shifted towards using more 'beautiful' models, which might be distressing to those identified as 'ugly'. Alternatively, instead of choosing a wholesome women's magazine, the author might have chosen a soft- or hardcore porn magazine for cover shot analysis; here the issue might be that of a woman who had perhaps been coerced into appearing for a cover shot in the 1970s but who subsequently bitterly regretted it and had sought to conceal her actions from her friends and family. Although works on non-fieldwork-based visual research methodology (e.g. Kress and van Leeuwen, 1996; van Leeuwen and Jewitt, 2001) do not generally contain explicit discussions of ethics, it is not hard to see that there is potentially an ethical dimension simply because in the reproduction of images for purposes of illustration or analysis, specific individuals can be identified.

Ethics and image-making

Ethical concerns are far more obviously to the fore when social researchers create their own images of research subjects, or use and reproduce essentially private images that they have supplied, such as family photographs. As noted in Chapters 1 and 3, the act of looking at people – scopophilia, the gaze, surveillance, snooping – can carry uneasy echoes of Foucault's panopticon model, especially when conducted by those who have or seek power over those so viewed. The power not simply to look, but to record and then disseminate, is a power that all social researchers who create images must reflexively address. There can be no absolute rules or guidelines about this (though writers such as Trinh T. Minh-ha come close to condemning all ethnographic film projects produced by 'white anthropology' (1991, cited in Ginsburg, 1999; see also Ruby, 2000, chap. 8).

At the time of image creation, when the social researcher brings out her camera and begins to film or take pictures, even if no formal permission has been sought or could easily be sought (for example, general scenes in a street or market), some people may not mind, but others may. The solution here is not so much a legal-ethical one (the researcher hands out release forms to everyone) but intellectual: the researcher should know enough about the society or community through her research, both in the library and in the field, to anticipate what the likely response will be. Similarly, at the time of reproduction and distribution of those images, a social researcher who cannot gauge what the response of her research subjects will be should question how much she really knows about the people. But once they have been taken and disseminated, a social researcher loses much control over the images, an issue to which I will return in the next chapter.

Apart from ceasing to film and photograph altogether, one useful solution to the problem of anonymity would seem to be to turn it on its head. Instead of worrying about the power of mechanical visual media inevitably to identify individuals and then seeking ways to curtail this, the answer would seem to be to explore and utilize this property. The collaborative film and video projects described above, and others like them, rest on an extended period of discussion with the subjects concerning the nature of visual representations and on encouraging subjects to use the media to express their voices (both literally and metaphorically). Such an approach is not necessarily limited to visual representations produced for sole or primary consumption within the community itself, but can just as easily be employed for films and photographic projects designed for consumption well away from the local context. The result should be that the voices heard are projected self-consciously, with permission for their use.

Permissions and copyright

Ethical issues are often intertwined with copyright and other legal issues,[30] and in theory the latter are generated by the former. In Euro-American societies, copyright in images is generally assigned to the image creator, not the image subject.[31] In the case of the magazine cover images discussed above the photographer would have held the copyright, not the models, although in this case the photographer would almost certainly have transferred the copyright to the magazine, which commissioned the images in the first place.

The principle is that by taking a photograph or a length of film or videotape, the creator brings something into being that did not previously exist and therefore has rights in it. The image subject by contrast has done nothing special beyond simply being. Unsurprisingly, not everyone agrees with this and some cases of what is sometimes called visual repatriation are discussed in the next chapter. Returning to the article on the magazine cover briefly discussed above, there is an argument that Bell, the author of the chapter, or his photographer could claim copyright in the two images of the covers in which they are laid out in a 4 x 5 grid (P. Bell, 2001, figs 2.1 and 2.2). This is an extremely grey area; the figures might count as 'derivative works' and if this were true then the copyright holder of the original magazine covers (the magazine's publishers presumably) could also claim copyright over the derivative work.

However, as Halpern argues, while copyright protects the expression of an idea (not the idea itself), quite what constitutes an 'expression' is open to argument (Halpern, 2003, pp. 152–3). Halpern goes on to consider the case of digital image manipulation: has a new thing been created, or is it still a derivative work? Some authors have been highly troubled by the advent of digital photography and its potential to undermine the 'truth' of images (e.g. Leslie, 1995), but others are more sanguine. Becker and Hagaman (the latter formerly a photojournalist), for example, point out that image manipulation has always taken place, in the sense of retouching, within journalism. What appears to be new is a concern with this, a concern that arises not from a moral or epistemological basis but from 'the unsettled and emerging social relations that constitute the worlds of image making today' (Becker and Hagaman, 2003, p. 349). In cases of copyright challenge the law is judging a set of conventions, not an ethical matter. Visual social researchers must therefore be alert to two issues. The first is legal: are they producing, reproducing or altering an image that someone else might claim to own? The second is moral: by what right (legally enforceable or otherwise) are they producing, reproducing or altering an image?

If negotiation and collaboration were advocated in the last section as one possible solution to the latter question, then permissions and release forms is one solution to the former question. As with solutions to ethical dilemmas, 'permission' has to be understood in a socially or culturally appropriate context. Some ethnographic and documentary filmmakers insist on using formal, written release forms or contracts with their subjects before filming; others do not and much writing has been devoted to the ethical rights and wrongs of documentary filmmaking (see Rosenthal, 1980; Gross et al., 1988). Amongst the media-literate, or in situations where a great deal of prior discussion takes place, the use of written release forms may well be possible and effective (Barbash and Taylor, 1997, pp. 485–7, provide templates for three release forms though they do advise consulting a lawyer). Amongst groups who have little familiarity with either literacy or mechanical image technologies such forms may be meaningless, or worse; people whose lives are blighted by officials waving documents, or those engaged in illegal activities, even if those activities are not captured on film, are likely to be hostile to signing their names to forms they barely understand.

It should be clear from all that I have said in this chapter that employing visual methodologies in 'real-world' fieldwork contexts is far from straightforward. The difficulties – such as ethical dilemmas – are best seen, however, as opportunities rather than barriers to be overcome. By engaging with research subjects about issues that matter to them in their lives, the quality of social research should be enhanced rather than diminished; a reflexive approach ('What does this research mean to me?') and a critical spirit of inquiry ('Whose interests are being served by this research?') are both deepened when the subjects of the research themselves ask such questions of the researcher.

Key points

- Ethnographic fieldwork is an intense and demanding process. Before undertaking it for the first time, researchers should attend all available training sessions and ideally speak to others who have done fieldwork, in order to be prepared as much as possible.
- It is quite possible that research subjects may be wary of having their photographs taken, or be upset to discover that photographs of them or their ancestors have been lodged in archives or libraries for anyone to look at. Researchers must be sensitive to local perceptions of photography and should always try and establish rapport with people before taking photographs or shooting video. Encouraging research subjects to take pictures with the researcher's camera is often a good way of breaking the ice and may lead to interesting results that feed into the research itself.
- As well as the broader ethical concerns that must be borne in mind, researchers must ascertain what particular legal constraints exist; in some countries, for example, it is illegal to take photographs of bridges or airports, in other countries, legal checks need to be made before a researcher can work with children or other vulnerable people. These checks can take some time, so it is wise to check what is required as soon as possible.

Further reading

Dresch et al. (2000) is not a methodological guide but provides some very useful insights into the practice of ethnographic fieldwork, while Ellen (1984), although now a little dated, is a good all-round guide to ethnographic practice; Nigel Fielding gives a more concise overview from a sociological perspective and also includes a discussion of covert research. Barbash and Taylor is the best guide to ethnographic film production and also includes useful sections on ethics and

(Continued)

permissions; both volumes by Gross et al. (1998, 2003) cover ethical issues in visual research from a wide range of perspectives. Collier and Collier, also now rather dated, is nonetheless helpful in providing background to visual methodologies such as photo-elicitation, while Pink covers a broader range, including new media practices. Angrosino gives an overview of ethnography, Kvale gives one of interviews, and Flick of issues of quality in qualitative research,

Angrosino, M. (2007). *Doing Ethnographic and Observational Research* (Book 3 of *The SAGE Qualitative Research Kit*). London: Sage.

Barbash, I. and Taylor, L. (1997) *Cross-Cultural Filmmaking: A Handbook for Making Documentary and Ethnographic Films and Videos*. Berkeley: University of California Press.

Collier, J. and Collier, M. (1986) *Visual Anthropology: Photography as a Research Method*. Albuquerque: University of New Mexico Press.

Dresch, P., James, W. and Parkin, D. (eds) (2000) *Anthropologists in a Wider World: Essays on Field Research*. Oxford: Berghahn Books.

Ellen, R.F. (ed.) (1984) *Ethnographic Research: A Guide to General Conduct*. London: Academic Press.

Fielding, N. (2001) 'Ethnography', in N. Gilbert (ed.), *Researching Social Life*. London: Sage, pp. 145–63.

Flick, U. (2007b) *Managing Quality in Qualitative Research* (Book 8 of *The SAGE Qualitative Research Kit*). London: Sage.

Gross, L., Katz, J. and Ruby, J. (eds) (1988) *Image Ethics: The Moral Rights of Subjects in Photographs, Film, and Television*. New York; Oxford: Oxford University Press.

Gross, L., Katz, J. and Ruby, J. (eds) (2003) *Image Ethics in the Digital Age*. Minneapolis: University of Minnesota Press.

Kvale, S. (2007) *Doing Interviews* (Book 2 of *The SAGE Qualitative Research Kit*). London: Sage.

Pink, S. (2001) *Doing Visual Ethnography: Images, Media and Representation in Research*. London: Sage.

5
Presenting visual research

Chapter objectives
After reading this chapter, you should

- understand that the audience should be considered before presenting research results;
- know a number of ways of presenting social research visually; and
- understand the examples that demonstrate the value of collaborative research.

Case study: *Oak park stories* **and mixed media presentation**

The recent work of visual anthropologist Jay Ruby provides an interesting example of using a full range of media to present and disseminate a social research project. Ruby has been examining social transformation in Oak Park, a Chicago suburb renowned for its social integration. To this end he conducted over a year of ethnographic fieldwork in Oak Park, during which he concentrated on several households that exemplify the suburb's social diversity, and on the housing centre and the schools that play a strong part in maintaining what Ruby calls '(the Oak Parkers') experiment in 'racial', economic, religious, and sexual diversity'. At this level the research is fairly conventional; what makes it distinctive is the methods Ruby has employed and the transparency and openness with which he has conducted it. At the start of the project Ruby set up a website, largely for the Oak Park residents themselves, explaining the aims and scope of the project.

(Continued)

FIGURE 5.1   Jay Ruby filming at the Oak Park Housing Center.
(courtesy of Oak Park Housing Center)

Over the course of the research Ruby has added to this website what now amounts to five years' worth of monthly and then quarterly progress reports, as well as draft academic papers, position statements on matters such as his funding applications, and stories about his work in the local newspaper.

Methodologically, Ruby was seeking to create what he calls 'a pictorial ethnography', which involved not only videotaping interviews and his research subjects' daily activities, but also amassing an archive of dozens of still photographs of Oak Park spanning over fifty years. He also sought to explore the limits of a reflexive and collaborative approach (he was himself born and raised in Oak Park) to social research. His chosen method of publication is on CD, which allows him to include still and moving images as well as text. It also allows him to present far more material then would be possible with a published book or a single ethnographic film, as well as freedom from the constraint of linearity, or creating a single coherent line of argument. Ruby embarked upon the project at about the time he retired from his academic post. In that sense, then, he had little to lose by choosing to 'publish' in a non-conventional way, while a younger researcher might feel under pressure to submit articles to peer-reviewed journals. However, his presentation of all his initial research materials and reports on an open website is a strategy that could be emulated by anyone, and is certainly conducive to promoting collaborative research (assuming the research subjects have Internet access and speak the language used on the website). Ruby's website for the project can be seen at http://astro.temple.edu/~ruby/opp/; the site also contains details of how to order the first two (of a projected four) *Oak Park Stories* CDs.

Modes of presentation

The previous chapter concluded with a discussion about ethics, rights and copyright and had therefore begun to move from a consideration of visual methods in the field, to a discussion of publication, presentation and dissemination. For the most part, social researchers present their findings in written form and disseminate them through conventional channels. There are, for example, at least four journals (listed at the end of Chapter 1) dedicated to publishing the results of social scientific visual research, and as visual methodologies spread from their original heartland in anthropology and sociology into areas such as psychology and health studies, journals in these disciplines are increasingly likely to accept submissions based on visual research. At the same time, students in at least some social science disciplines are able to conduct visual research at doctoral level (and below) and to have their findings accepted by their peers and examiners. The majority of such publications (or dissertations) reproduce visual materials created or studied during the course of the research, but these typically have an illustrative function and are intended to support or give evidence for the written argument, not provide a counter-argument. There are of course exceptions; for example, Rose's *Visual Methodologies* (2001) and Emmison and Smith's *Researching the Visual* (2000) both contain images that the reader is asked to work with in some way, but then both these texts are aimed at students and have a didactic intent. The present volume by contrast uses the small number of images almost entirely for illustrative purposes.

Whatever the aim of the images used, the chief considerations (at least for publications, rather than student dissertations[32]) are to do with copyright and reproduction rights, and cost. Apart from these considerations, the dissemination of visual research results in this way differs little from the dissemination of any research results. By contrast, in this chapter I am largely concerned with the *visual* presentation of research results, and not the presentation of visual research results in written or verbal form.

Understanding the audience

As with any research project, visual research projects need to consider the intended audience(s) from the outset, but perhaps need to be especially mindful of unintended audiences too. There are also distinctive issues to consider when presenting the results of visual research, particularly when presenting them visually (in whole or in part). That images are multivocal, and 'speak' to different people in different contexts in different ways, is an axiom of visual research itself; if – somehow – this were not the case, then most visual research would be rendered redundant. Yet it sometimes seems as if social researchers presenting their results visually do not consider this point sufficiently.

For example, the small amount of research done on the reception of documentary films by audiences shows that they do not transparently and naturally read the films, but bring to them previously formed social and cultural understandings. In research conducted on American student audiences, viewing films as part of an introductory anthropology course, Martinez found that certain films would generate an aberrant response, a 'misreading' of the films' supposed intentions (Martinez, 1990, 1992). In films about exotic research subjects, such as forest-dwelling Amerindians, the students 'read' the appearance and behaviour of the subjects (nearly naked, and performing elaborate ceremonies, sometimes linked to threats of warfare or violence) as confirmation of the inaccurate stereotypes they already held of 'primitive' or 'tribal' people. Similarly, films that had an explicitly didactic intent, with voiceover commentary and on-screen tables or diagrams, were thought to be dry and boring. Following Umberto Eco, Martinez roughly categorizes film texts as open or closed. The more didactic or 'closed' a text is, the more likely it is to miss its target and be subject to aberrant readings. Conversely, 'open' films – loosely structured, observational in style, free of commentary – are more successful, demanding as they do a greater involvement on the part of the viewer in order to make sense of the text (Martinez, 1992, pp. 135–6). More anecdotally, Ginsburg notes that while a professional filmmaker and post-colonial critic has dismissed Worth and Adair's 'Through Navajo Eyes' project (1972) as 'patronizing', Native American students whom Ginsburg has taught find it 'both compelling and valuable' (Ginsburg, 1999, p. 162).

These findings are context-specific, relating in both instances to US student audiences. The point, however, is that whatever the image producer intends as the 'correct' reading of a film or other image, the audience may respond to it in other, but not necessarily random, ways.

Presenting visual research in academic contexts

Many social researchers conduct their work within an academic environment and are expected to acquire the skills and learn the conventions by which such research is presented to an academic audience. With respect to written research findings, these conventions are relatively well established, though they differ from discipline to discipline and also change over time. With respect to visual communications, however, whatever skills a researcher may have (in film editing, for example), the conventions to which she should conform are far less well defined. In tune with the anthropologist Margaret Mead's claim that the social sciences are 'disciplines of words' (Mead, 1995), some visual social researchers have suggested that their work is neither understood nor properly appreciated by their professional colleagues (e.g. Grady, 1991; Prosser, 1998). As noted in Chapter 2, after an early period in which photography was accepted as 'evidence' of sociological claims, the power of the image in anthropology and sociology quickly waned and for the most part photographs tend to appear in written studies merely as illustrations, relatively redundant additions to the text.[33] Moving images cannot be integrated into printed texts at all, of course (but see below on multimedia), but for ethnographic film at least a rich circuit of ethnographic film festivals has developed since the 1970s that allows them to be presented to professional anthropologists and filmmakers alike.

Even when used as 'mere' illustrations in an essentially word-oriented text, tied down by captions and text that describes the image, photographs and other images in academic publications are not easily constrained, especially as time passes or context changes. This is most certainly true of early publications in the 'races of mankind' genre, where, divorced from the intellectual assumptions of the day, it is now difficult to see the supposed typology that the images were supposed to demonstrate. In the previous chapter it was proposed that the best way to deal with ethical and intellectual issues arising from visual research was to work *with* research subjects rather than work *on* them. In a parallel fashion in their presentation of visual research, researchers might seek to work with images, to let them speak for themselves as it were, rather than trying to force them to conform to a predetermined intellectual agenda. This idea will be explored further in the section below on multimedia; see also the case study at the start of this chapter.

Presenting stills: the photographic essay

In the previous chapter I briefly described how Ruud van Wezel worked with his research subjects in Lisbon to create a *fotonovella*, a presentational form that was familiar to the subjects yet with new content. Although this particular form would not be familiar to most academics, most will be familiar with photo-journalism, and many will recognize the photographic essay. Photographic essays originated as a form of journalism, and though perhaps less common today they can still be found occasionally in weekend newspaper supplements or as gallery exhibitions. While theoretically they can be devoted to any subject, historically there has been a particular bias towards matters of social policy and social concern. From the 1960s the art critic/social critic John Berger and photographer Jean Mohr collaborated on a series of projects that effectively transcended the boundaries between serious journalism, social criticism and sociology, examining the British middle classes (1967), migrants in Europe (1975) and European peasants (1982), thus introducing the form into the academic arena. More recently, journals such as *Critique of Anthropology*, *Visual Communication* and *Visual Sociology* (now *Visual Studies*) have published article-length photographic essays, and a few authors have been able to convince publishers to publish book-length photographic essays (for example, Harper, 1982, 1987b), or to include visual essays in book-length works (for example, Danforth and Tsiaras, 1982).

In an article on constructing what he calls visual ethnographic narratives, Harper outlines two modes of sequencing still photographs that would be appropriate for the construction of a photographic essay (Harper, 1987a). In the phenomenological mode, an attempt is made to present the subjective experience of some social phenomena from both the researcher's and insiders' perspectives. While obviously guided by some kind of narrative, strict chronological sequence need not be adhered to, the aim is exploratory and the overall effect is cumulative; the end result is intended to 'create the experience of process, to evoke a feeling of tone and texture of entering another culture' (1987a, p. 4). In contrast, the narrative mode, for which Harper identifies a large number of photographic essays and ethnographic films, is more concerned with telling a story, a story in which the researcher may have participated, but that nonetheless is primarily the story of the research subjects.

Some might claim that the job of empirical sociology is not to tell stories but to employ survey and other methods to gather data in a systematic fashion and then present the results in an unambiguous and precise way. Refuting this, visual sociologist John Grady presents two counter-arguments. First, quantitative or formalist sociological approaches do not completely encompass all the relevant material; quite apart from what is excluded from the research frame, even within it there is the problem of residual indeterminacy, the data items that do not fit after all the rest have been neatly categorized. Secondly, all textual accounts of research are inevitably narrativized anyway (Grady, 1991, pp. 29, 34). To this we might add, following Pink (2001, p. 135), that no one is suggesting that photographic essays completely replace all other modes of social research presentation, but that there are forms of critical ethnography that are particularly well served by visual (re)presentation. This is particularly true when a form of social life is well known through its visual representations; Pink cites the example of Schwartz's work on the Minneapolis Superbowl, where the images taken by Schwartz act as a counterpoint to the image of the event 'manufactured' by its creators and sponsors (Schwartz, 1993, cited in Pink, 2001, p. 135).

There is no single model for a photographic essay, and social researchers considering this form of research presentation should look at a range of existing examples to consider the variations possible. In all cases perhaps the most important issue to think through is the relationship between images and text. Some researchers choose to caption the images, while others do not. But when captioning, should the captions be lengthily descriptive and perhaps interpretive, or merely confined to factual data such as date and location? If captions are not used, should the images at least be numbered (Figure 1, Figure 2, etc.) and cited in the accompanying text, or simply left to speak for themselves? Should there be any accompanying text at all, whether or not the images are captioned? The answers to these questions depend in part on what the social researcher is trying to do with the presentation, but also in part on whom she considers the audience to be. Within anthropology, for example, a researcher cannot readily assume that the readership will have knowledge of the broad ethnographic context of which the specific ethnography presented through the photographs forms a detailed part, and so some accompanying text or quite lengthy captions are normally called for. Alternatively, a written text can present relatively factual material, perhaps even the results of quantitative analysis that would be readily understood by a specialist sociological readership, while the uncaptioned images can act as an expressive counterpart.

The aim in general is to ensure that text and image are deployed in such a way as to maximize their communicative or expressive potential. In this way, the photographic essay is rather different from an illustrated text. In their book on 'the grammar of visual design', Kress and van Leeuwen (1996) present over 180 images in the course of 280 or so pages, but the vast majority of these are intended to be illustrative examples of a point made in the text or are presentations of their source material. The images are not intended to be read independently of the text or to form a meta-argument of their own, but are instead constrained by the text to perform a particular function. By contrast, the photographic essay at the end of Danforth and Tsiaras's book on Greek death rituals (1982) forms a parallel text both to the main written text and to the individual accompanying texts; the images are intended to go beyond and to provide a counterpoint to the words.

Presenting film and video

In this section I am concerned only with films made by social researchers with the specific intent of making a contribution to their disciplinary practice and findings; I therefore exclude what is probably the majority of 'ethnographic' films. This is not to deny the value of such films – about which I and others have written extensively – but simply to retain the focus on social research first and foremost. Films that are specifically conceived and executed as part of an ongoing process of social research generate specific considerations of audience.

The French anthropologist and ethnographic filmmaker Jean Rouch once said that he made films first of all for himself, secondly for the people who participated in the films, and finally for 'the greatest number of people, for everyone' (Eaton, 1979, p. 44–6). While such an order of priority is a luxury that perhaps only the tenacious (like Rouch) or the independently wealthy social researcher can afford, his statement is a reminder that the audiences for visual research may be multiple. I deal below with the second of Rouch's audiences, the research subjects, and focus here on the third.[34] While having 'the greatest number of people' viewing one's film is a desirable goal, in practice, the vast majority of films made by social researchers are seen by a few dozen people at a film festival or two, and from then on are largely seen by students to whom they are shown for didactic purposes.[35]

Films made by professional filmmakers, on topics of broad sociological concern, are frequently intended for television screening, whether or not a professional social researcher was involved in the production. In this context, there are claims that such films can serve to advertise a discipline, such as anthropology, and its findings to a lay audience, and thereby promote greater tolerance or understanding. There is some anecdotal evidence that this may be true, but further research is needed to demonstrate this effect. The work of Martinez, cited at the start of this chapter, indicates that the opposite effect is also a possible outcome.

But to claim that students will probably form the largest audience for a social researcher's film is not intended to denigrate either the film or student audiences. A great deal of written research output is read by students, as well as of course by fellow professionals and practitioners. As the majority of undergraduate students in social research disciplines will not stay on to become professional sociologists or anthropologists or whatever, then it is important that the books and papers they read and the films they see during their studies are well considered and their sociological insights clear. This is not to say that all films should be didactic, but an awareness of the broader context of viewing should play a part. Professional filmmakers, with an eye on a television audience, are under no obligation and perhaps have little interest in ensuring the sociological validity of their productions. Professional social researchers, in the knowledge that students will almost certainly view their work, should be as concerned that it articulates with the broader corpus of social research in the relevant area as they would be in preparing a paper for publication.

This is not to advocate a slavish conformity, so that all social research films merely confirm or illustrate familiar sociological positions. Following the line of Grimshaw, mentioned in the previous chapter, the deployment of visual methodologies may well challenge existing positions within a discipline, but they can only do so in full knowledge of what those positions are. In the course of planning and then executing a social research film project it is necessary to tread a middle ground between a 'something for everyone' approach towards the intended audience and too narrow a focus on a specific audience. The former runs the risk of engaging no one very strongly, the latter runs the risk of missing its particular target. The heavily didactic films that Martinez found were susceptible to aberrant readings had been created for use in teaching anthropology to North American college students of the late 1960s. Whatever their reception then, a later generation found them 'boring and repetitious' and 'didn't understand what was happening' (Martinez, 1990, p. 41).

As with the photographic essay, the relationship between image and text must also be considered. Heavily didactic films normally feature a nearly constant voiceover narration, which describes what the viewer can see on the screen or directs the viewer's attention to particular incidents or actions. More 'open' films, those that require the viewer to engage with the images and sound to seek meaning, have little or nothing in the way of a voiceover. There are advantages and disadvantages to both positions; in the latter case especially, there is a danger that 'open' films about exotic (to the viewer) research subjects lack sufficient contextualization for the viewer to make sense of what they are seeing and hearing.

For this reason, some writers on ethnographic film have advocated the production of study guides to accompany films used in teaching (e.g. Heider, 1976, p. 127). Although there is disagreement about this, to some extent it is a non-issue. Whether or not a specific study guide is produced, a film created and presented as an outcome of a piece of social research will not be the sole output; there will be reports, a dissertation, published papers, conference presentations and other forms of written and language-based output. Taken together these form a corpus of research results, each part making its own point but each supporting or adding alternative perspectives to the others.

Professional acceptance

Students usually have little choice about what, and how, they are taught. The screening of an ethnographic film or a slide show may provide an hour or so of welcome relief from a talk-based lecture series and the effective use of visual materials in teaching can be evaluated in post-course response surveys, but on the whole students are not expected to pass judgement on the intellectual contribution of visual research results to social research disciplines such as anthropology and sociology. Some professional visual researchers are, however, concerned about evaluation by their peers, particularly when it comes to matters of hiring or promotion, and worry that they are not taken seriously by their colleagues, that their work is neither understood nor properly appreciated (e.g. Grady, 1991; Prosser, 1998; but cf. MacDougall, 1997). In response to this, particularly with regard to employment and research track-records, the Society for Visual Anthropology (a section of the American Anthropological Association) has issued a set of guidelines for the evaluation of 'ethnographic visual media' to aid university hiring committees (SVA, 2001).

Although the guidelines relate specifically to the discipline of anthropology, they can with thought be adapted to other social research disciplines. They carry no legal weight of course, and hiring and promotion committees are under no obligation to consult them, but they act as a useful starting point in ensuring the professional acceptance of non-print research outcomes. The guidelines stress two broad points. First, that not all sociological knowledge of society can be presented in written form and that 'visual representations offer viewers a means to experience and understand ethnographic complexity, richness and depth' (SVA, 2001, p. 5). Secondly, that the production of non-print research materials is by no means a trivial task – 'independent of preparatory fieldwork, the creation of a film easily consumes forty hours for every minute of screen time' (SVA, 2001, p. 6).

The guidelines urge committees to consider these and other points (such as the value of audiovisual media in teaching) when considering the research output of a scholar, which may be light on traditional published works, but heavy with films, photographic exhibitions and multimedia productions. The guidelines also suggest that committees seek advice from professional visual media specialists and that those being evaluated present letters of support from external experts such as members of film festival juries. The guidelines do not advocate uncritical acceptance of visual media research outputs – after all, the forty hours of preparation for one minute of screen time may have resulted in a film that is sociologically naïve or that is technically deficient – but simply seek to ensure that unfamiliar modes of research presentation are not dismissed simply because of their unfamiliarity.

Presenting visual research to research subjects

The emphasis I gave to collaborative research projects in the previous chapter finds its corollary in the decision to present visual research results to the original research subjects. The moral justification for this should be obvious: the research subjects gave their time and commitment to the project, often without remuneration, and it is only fair that they should see the results. The cost of making copies of photographs or videotapes to give to research subjects should be an essential component of a research budget. Questions of 'ownership' of the images should also be established early on in the research process.

There are also intellectual justifications for sharing visual results with research subjects. Several examples have already been mentioned in previous chapters: Collier showed his photographs of the weaving process to the weaver only to be told he had misunderstood and misrepresented (Collier and Collier, 1986); Steiger (1995) and van der Does and her colleagues (1992) took photographs of or with research subjects, then used these as the basis for interviews, followed by further photographing sessions, and so on. In this section I discuss a number of ways in which visual research results can be shared or returned, indicating the sometimes unanticipated problems that can ensue (see also Barbash and Taylor, 1997, pp. 6–9).

Exhibitions

At the conclusion of some research projects it is obvious which images should be offered to which people. Where small numbers of research subjects are involved, and the researcher is creating her own images (as with Collier, Steiger and van der Does), the images may be of interest only to those featured in them. The images may also be sufficiently intimate that the featured subjects might be uncomfortable with them being more widely seen. In the course of other projects the images used are historical or are more distantly connected to specific research subjects and several researchers have decided instead to mount a public exhibition. In one case, Joshua Bell, an anthropologist, took two collections of historical photographs to villages in the Purari Delta of Papua New Guinea and used a variety of means to show the prints to the villagers. The point of taking the images to the Purari Delta was to allow Bell access to historical narratives needed for his research. The images themselves were created by two sets of anthropologists in the early decades of the twentieth century and were received 'with overwhelming enthusiasm' (J. Bell, 2003, p. 115). Bell describes the noisy and chaotic scenes when he showed the images to groups of people, as well as the more measured – and sometimes contradictory – responses from individuals who viewed the images privately. On at least one occasion he mounted an impromptu exhibition simply by thumb-tacking the images (digital laser copies) to the outside wall of a reed house and letting people make their own minds up about when and in whose company to view and comment on the pictures (Bell, personal communication). Displaying the images publicly and listening to the responses, but also showing them privately in the course of conversation, allowed Bell to see that the villagers' history was contested, subject to revision, and intimately tied up with political events in the present.

Similar serendipitous circumstances led Geffroy and a co-researcher to mount an exhibition of old photographs in a village in the south of France (Geffroy, 1990). As briefly discussed in the previous chapter, Geffroy had been conducting research on the history of a popular saint's day festival when he realized the value of photo-elicitation to augment his knowledge of the village's past. During the course of the research, Geffroy and his colleague gathered a large number of old photographs but realized they lacked basic information concerning the people, places and events depicted in many cases. Consequently, they arranged for an exhibition of the photographs to be mounted in which they displayed the photographs side by side with a line-drawing outline of the compositional elements. Visitors to the exhibition were asked to supply whatever information they could by writing on the outlines, which they did, as well as supplying yet more photographs. Not only did the researchers gather more data for their work on social memory, Geffroy describes how the experience affected the villagers themselves:

> (the exhibition) created an atmosphere of excitement in Utelle: new meetings, intergenerational exchanges, discussions, and *veillées* (evening social gatherings in private houses) took place. During the exhibition, it was not unusual to see people, photographs in hand, either meeting in the street or crossing the village to a friend or relative's house. (1990, p. 376)

In some sense, the actions of Geffroy and his colleague inadvertently stimulated a return to earlier forms of social interaction, bringing the village society into chronological conformity – however transiently – with the images themselves.

As with all other aspects of the research process, there are ethical issues to consider, as well as questions of legal and moral ownership of the images. Geffroy, above, was exhibiting images that the villagers owned anyway but had kept stashed away in their homes. Bell, in contrast, was presenting the Purari Delta villagers with images they had never seen before yet with which they strongly identified. Ethical and ownership issues, while always present, come to the fore when images are 'repatriated' to their source communities in this way.

Visual repatriation

Within the museum world generally, and the world of the ethnographic museum specifically, questions surrounding repatriation have been vigorously discussed in recent years. Although the issue of the British Museum's continued retention of the Parthenon ('Elgin') Marbles has been in public and professional consciousness for many decades, since the 1960s the growing strength of the indigenous rights movement means that many ethnographic museums must now reconsider their ownership and display of objects acquired, by whatever means, by previous generations of collectors. In many cases, the relationship between collector and what have come to be called source communities formed part of a broader colonial relationship (Peers and Brown, 2003). Setting aside the complex practical, political and moral issues involved in discussions about repatriating objects from museum collections, it is perhaps rather glib – yet true – to point out that it is quite straightforward to return copies of photographs and film footage held in museum collections and archives. Photomechanically produced images can be copied relatively easily and the copies 'repatriated' in a variety of forms: as high-quality studio prints, as digital images on CD (perhaps for use in a local cultural centre), or simply as laser prints from digitized copies as Bell did.

The imperative to 'repatriate' in this way may be a moral end in itself – to return that which was taken – but it may also be a form of research strategy, as it was in Bell's case.[36] The naïve researcher might assume that local communities would receive repatriated images from their ancestral past unconditionally and with gratitude – a welcome return of their 'visual heritage', as Geffroy terms it (1990). Though this can happen (see Kingston, 2003, for an example) it should not be presumed, and while the sometimes unexpected or even hostile reception given to returned images may be uncomfortable for the social researcher in the field, there are also valuable sociological insights to be gained from observing and analyzing the process. For example, it might be expected that different generations of a community would react differently to seeing images of their ancestors. An oral history project that involved the return of images to a group of Luo people in Kenya found that while younger people were at ease with the images, older people were rather embarrassed by the 'primitive' appearance of their forefathers (Edwards, 2003, p. 98 n. 3). Conversely, Bell found that while older people in the Purari Delta generally reacted favourably to the photographs he showed them, some younger men distanced themselves from the images and laughed at them (J. Bell, 2003, p. 116).

The differences are not so much explained by the differing historical trajectories of the two groups, but rather a way to learn more about those historical trajectories. In the Purari Delta case, the villagers had varying and ambiguous opinions regarding a local man who, after the Second World War, radically disrupted their society through a social movement that introduced new styles of living and a new faith (Baha'i). As the images showed Purari life before the Kabu Movement, their examination caused the villagers to question their own contemporary life, including their troubled relationship with two Malaysian logging companies operating in the Delta. The photographs were thus not received unproblematically and through their reception a complex web of contemporary social relationships was inscribed into the past. For Bell, the image repatriation allowed him access to subtleties of Purari Delta social relations that, one suspects, he simply would not have been aware of otherwise.

The repatriation of visual images can be performed by individual social researchers and may be relatively trouble-free, especially if the researcher is a member of or already linked to the source community (as was Deanna Paniataaq Kingston, who 'returned' a documentary film from the 1930s to the King Island Native community in Alaska to which she was maternally related: Kingston, 2003). On the whole, however, such projects are best undertaken as part of a series of ongoing discussions and exchanges between metropolitan museums and archives and source communities. Thought should also be given to what members of the source community are supposed to do with the images. Stanton reports that Aboriginal families in Kimberly lacked the technology (and older people lacked the skills) to make any use of CD-ROMs of repatriated images from the Berndt Museum in Western Australia, and preferred instead to have albums of prints (Stanton, 2003, p. 145). Although Brown and Peers did create CD-ROMs of historical images of the Kainai Nation in Alberta, Canada, these were prepared for use in schools as part of a broader cultural policy agreed upon by the Kainai Nation (cited in Edwards, 2003, p. 94).

In all the projects described in this section above, the images could well have been studied in isolation, by the social researcher, as historical documents. Using content analysis, or perhaps a psychoanalytical approach,[37] the researchers could have devoted themselves to a reading of the images' internal narrative, perhaps complemented by an assessment of the historical context at the time of image production. Instead, all the researchers cited above chose to identify a new audience for the images – the subjects of the photographs themselves (or their descendants) – and to undertake field research that brought images and subjects together. In so doing, not only were new readings of the photographs – and indeed photography itself – brought to the fore, but new insights into the social relations of the communities under study were generated.

Digital and multimedia presentations

Over the past decade or so there has been a growing enthusiasm among visual social researchers for computer-based systems that allow images, sound and text to be combined in ways previously not possible with traditional analogue media. Once digitized, images can be stored, copied and transmitted with no loss of quality.[38] They can be output to a variety of media – television screens and VDUs, photographic paper, ordinary paper, and so on. Sound, text and moving images can all be treated in much the same way and, more importantly, linked to and combined with each other. In the abstract, then, computer-based systems seem to overcome many of the intellectual issues and practical problems highlighted earlier in this chapter. Multiple copies of a film can be made, for example, some with voiceover commentary, some without, for different audiences. Images and text can be combined in multiple ways to present or withhold captions. Study guides and other associated materials can be stored together with a film. Audiences can create their own 'pathways' through a series of still images to make multiple photo essays.

Although there are important exceptions, many multimedia productions (on the web or CD) are self-published, financed by grants or perhaps from the social researcher's own pocket. There are advantages and disadvantages to this. The chief advantages are that as much material as desired can be 'published' in this way. Few commercial and even non-commercial publishers would sanction more than a dozen or so photographic reproductions in a book, for example, especially one written by a young or first-time scholar, while a CD or website could include thousands if desired. In addition, the researcher has full control over the placement of images, their relation (if any) to text, and numerous other factors of layout and design that publishers might not understand or find too costly to implement. The downside of self-publishing is first that such productions are rarely if ever peer-reviewed or subject to careful editing, and secondly that distribution is normally extremely limited. Even if published on the web and therefore universally distributed, a piece of visual social research must still be brought to the attention of fellow researchers and others if it is to make an impact.

Multimedia publication differs in some significant ways from conventional print-on-paper publication, though as Sarah Pink notes, there are several examples in the field of social research that could essentially have been printed in the conventional way (2001, p. 159). Fischer and Zeitlyn (n.d.) liken this use of multimedia to a film, something that unfolds sequentially before the viewer, such as a PowerPoint presentation. A slightly more ambitious use of the medium still retains an overall structure and a sequence, but hyperlinks carry the user sideways, as it were, to the equivalent of footnotes. Visual anthropologists have increasingly been attracted to the possibilities this model opens up for adding visual and textual 'footnotes' to ethnographic films; the model is one of a principal text with associated subtexts.

Amazonia in multimedia

A particularly rich example of a core text and subsidiary texts model is seen in Biella, Chagnon and Seaman's *Yanomamo Interactive*, a multimedia re-working of a well-known ethnographic film, much used in teaching (Biella et al., 1997). In 1975 filmmaker Tim Asch and anthropologist Napoleon Chagnon completed a film, *The Ax Fight,* about a brief but violent dispute that occurred in a village of Amazonian Yanomamo people in Venezuela, where they were working. The fight took place without warning, at least to the visitors, and they struggled to get themselves ready to film it; the film opens with only the soundtrack, for example, as the sound recordist was able get his equipment up and running before the camera operator.

Faced with 11 minutes or so of raw footage, over which they had had almost no shooting control or preparation, Asch and Chagnon edited the finished film into a three-part structure. First, there is the original footage, which plunges the viewer into the raw experience of the event with as little preparation as the filmmakers had; then, there is an analytical section in which some of the original footage, stills taken from it, and genealogical diagrams are edited together with an explanatory commentary outlining exactly which participant did what to whom, and why; finally, the original sequence is played again, edited lightly for smoothness but without commentary, allowing the viewer to put the knowledge imparted in the previous section to make more sense of the sequence of events as they unfold. A multimedia, or certainly a multimodal logic is clearly at work here, but constrained by the linear time-based unfolding of the film itself.

Twenty years later Biella and colleagues were able to unlock this potential in the film by transferring it, and many associated texts, to a digital format. The film forms the 'core text' and can be played from the CD in full (albeit in a tiny window). But it has been broken down into its constituent shots, each of which can be played separately, accompanied by a text of the relevant narration. By way of the 'footnotes' to the core text, a large number of written texts have been added – the narration track, a number of essays, a written scene-by-scene description – together with numerous still photographs of the Yanomamo villagers involved and genealogical diagrams showing how they are related. At any point in viewing the film, the viewer can break out and explore a number of issues in depth. In this way, the integrity of the original research material is preserved, as is the original analysis (as encoded in the original film and Chagnon's writings), but the validity of that analysis can now be placed under scrutiny, raising the possibility of alternative analyses.

Fischer and Zeitlyn also identify a form that they term a layered model: a set of objects are linked to one another horizontally (metaphorically speaking) such as a sequence of video clips, or passages of text, but the layers are also linked vertically (again, metaphorically), so that an image in one layer may be linked to a passage of text in another, and on to a graph or bar chart in another, and so on. An example of such a structure is outlined by Coover (2004b) in his description of a CD-ROM project he created. In a section of a much larger piece, concerned with the grape harvest in Burgundy, a horizontal sequence of photographs – a layer – runs over several horizontally sequenced passages of text (see also Coover, 2004a). The piece was initially conceived as an aid to structuring a documentary film but can stand in its own right as another way of structuring a report of the research process, one that in this case includes a reflexive text layer about the shooting process itself, as well as text layers concerning the harvest and the winemaker (Coover, 2004b, pp. 187–8).

East Africa in multimedia

A rather more complex approach to the layering process is seen at work in a piece still under construction at the time of writing. In the early 1990s anthropologist Wendy James acted as consultant to a television ethnographic film on the Uduk people of Sudan, with whom she had been working for many years. At one point during the research and shooting, a fight broke out in the refugee camp where the Uduk were staying.[39] Although the incident, and subsequent reflections on it, were filmed by the crew, the sequence was not included in the final film for various reasons. James, however, felt that the material provided valuable insight into the construction and representation of emotional states, in this case fear, and wrote an article presenting the material and her analysis of it (James, 1997). However, she was not convinced that the article was able to do justice to her data (many of which were visual). Consequently she began a collaboration with an anthropologist and multimedia producer, Judith Aston, to try and bring the analytical insights of the article together with the original filmed material, a collaboration that forms the basis of a case study for Aston's doctoral research on multimedia use in anthropology (Aston, 2003). Working with what were essentially found materials – the original article and the film footage, supplemented with additional film footage, still photographs and sound recordings created by James on other occasions – the task Aston set herself was to retain the analytical insight and argument of the written text, to make full use of the sensory richness of the film and soundtrack, and to exploit the potential of digital multimedia to greatest effect.

In the relevant chapter of her report (Aston, 2003, chap. 7) Aston describes four iterations of the process, ranging from a simple division of the original article into sections interspersed with relevant video clips (Fischer and Zeitlyn's 'film' model of sequential unfolding), through two versions that come close to the 'core text and footnotes' model, to the latest, but not necessarily final, model, where for certain elements a 'vertical' rather than a 'horizontal' layering effect can be seen. For example, James and Aston had footage and sound material that

107

provided three different perspectives on the violent incident that James had witnessed: from an Uduk person, from a United Nations representative, and from a member of another ethnic group in the refugee camp. The three clips are arranged side by side on the screen, allowing the user to move back and forth between the perspectives. In another instance, in seeking to present James's original point that time has a distancing effect on the recollection of strong emotional states, such as fear, Aston again provides three contrasting video clips side by side. This time, three individuals recount their fears and experiences of fear: in one case a woman tells of her brother who had recently been shot by rebel soldiers, in another a woman describes her daughter who had disappeared some time earlier, in the third a man remembers an outbreak of worry and concern among the Uduk people some time back. Aston provides a control bar for the three video clips allowing them to be viewed individually or all at once, with the ability to freeze any of them and make frame-by-frame comparisons (Aston, 2003, pp. 183–4).

Such vertically layered sequences in the Uduk project, including others that demonstrate continuity over time as well as change, are themselves presented against other, horizontal layers, creating a web-like effect, but one where Aston is continually struggling to balance, as she puts it, 'authorial control with user agency' (Aston, 2003, p. 189). This issue, of offering the user the opportunity to roam freely around a set of digital texts – sound, print, image – and yet allowing the author to retain some kind of coherent argument or process of analysis, lies at the heart of much thinking about the use of multimedia to present the findings of social research. 'Layered' multimedia, where the layers are linked by multiple hypermedia links, has great potential, allowing the user to explore their own lines of inquiry through the material. Linear presentations, such as a film or an article, in contrast allow the researcher to present her material in support of a dominant narrative or single line of argument that the user/reader/viewer must follow in sequence. The carefully thought-out progression towards a conclusion would be undermined if a user could jump through the material in any order they wished.

Aston concludes that an optimal balance and hence a resolution to this tension has yet to be achieved in many projects (Aston, 2003, p. 198), although she suggests that in contemporary anthropology at least, multiple points of view and alternative explanations can be advanced without fundamentally undermining the authority of the researcher. Certainly in planning multimedia productions it would be a rejection of the value of social research itself if an author were to offer an 'anything goes' approach to the user. It would also be disingenuous; if, as suggested at the start of Chapter 3, no social researcher comes to the research process without some kind of tacit theoretical approach, then the same holds true for the presentation of research results. A particular analytical approach is inevitably implied, and good multimedia productions should be able to acknowledge that while at the same time presenting both the evidence from which it is derived as well as that which might allow for alternative interpretations.

Materiality in multimedia

Another point arising from Aston's study returns us rather unexpectedly to a matter raised towards the end of Chapter 3, concerning the materiality of images. Most social researchers have a sense of what kind of time commitment is involved in reading a book or watching a film. These linear media allow a relatively quick judgement of how the piece is structured and where the weight and emphasis lie: one can flick through a book, consult the index and contents page (both forms of hypermedia navigation) and form a rough assessment of how much time (in the form of words) is devoted to each subtopic. Even with a film, one can keep an eye on the clock to gain a sense of how soon the end is coming and therefore how much time will be left for tying up the narrative threads.

However, this kind of 'at a glance' information is rarely available to multimedia users: a CD-ROM disk, or even worse, a website front page, can be extremely uninformative about what lies within. Aston proposes some solutions to this problem such as, for example, indicating how many pages of text (or minutes of video) are called up by a navigation button (2003, p. 173). Similarly, site maps and detailed menus or tables of contents can also help to give a user a sense of scope and weighting, but possibly at the cost of removing some of the immediacy that makes multimedia so attractive to creators and users. Finally, until a user has worked her way through the whole multimedia project, she will be unable to gain a sense of just how interactive it turned out to be – which links were enabled and which were not between the various layers. This last point is dependent in part on the approach taken to coding by the original author(s).

Organizing images and other data

Before they can be assembled into a multimedia presentation, social researchers need to organize the images, texts, sound files and other data items they have gathered in the course of their research. Of course, this is true whether or not digital or multimedia presentation is intended as the mode of output, but is especially necessary when it is. Written materials – field notes, interview transcripts, texts produced by research subjects – once digitized either by re-keying or by scanning and optical character recognition, can be coded and organized in a variety of ways. At the most basic level such texts can be stored as simple word processor files and searched using the 'find' routine.

More sophisticated, and powerful, procedures involve either tagging lexical items with unique codes, or distributing parts of a text across the fields of a database. In these ways, idiosyncrasies and variant vocabulary can be overcome – a reference to 'rice fields' in one part of a researcher's field notes should receive the same code as a reference to 'paddy fields' in another part of the notes, for example. Coding and breaking text up into database fields has to be done by hand, of course, and a computer cannot understand the significance of what has been done. Nonetheless, once it has been done and depending on the software program used, the computer can perform sophisticated searches, for example, 'find all occurrences of the [code for] "paddy-or-rice field" within fifty words of the [codes for] "communal labour" and "women" but ignore any text item dated after [code for] "January 2001"'. While the computer and the software have no comprehension of the meaning of any of these terms, together they recognize patterns denoting lexical strings or items.[40] This is not true for images, however.

Computers cannot 'see' except in very prescribed instances where pattern matching is possible, for example in automated fingerprint or iris striation recognition systems. The vast majority of still images used or created by social researchers do not conform to such narrow visual parameters. Consequently, while image digitization creates a file of code apparently similar to that of a text file, the difficulty of isolating sections of this code that correspond to elements of the image is great and even then the software has no way to understand that all elements so identified (for example, as 'women') are the 'same' thing, such that it can automatically identify new ones.

Put another way, while software exists that can 'read' printed or even handwritten text, identifying letters of the alphabet, punctuation and spacing, there is no reliable software that can 'read' images and identify houses, people, pots and pans, or whatever. Image databanks therefore rely on meta-data, input by the researcher or user, that essentially mimic photographic captions. The creator can decide upon a number of relatively unproblematic categories, such as place, date, names of individuals present, but is still going to have to make interpretive decisions concerning other matters: is it a photograph of a group of women and children, for example, or a photograph of 'child-rearing' (an abstract category)?

The problems are exponentially magnified when moving images are considered. Such problems of interpretation and abstraction apply to text as well; the words 'paddy field', 'women', 'communal labour' and 'January 2001' are all easily identified, but the concept that links them – for example, 'the gender composition of communal labour parties in the rice fields prior to changes brought about through price structure reforms in 2001' – is an analytical addition of the database user. There are numerous coding schemes for textual analysis, in which the more abstract and interpretive meta-data are arranged in some kind of logical order (for example, 'formal education' as a subcategory of 'socialization'), but while these can be applied to the content of an image, moving or still, they still do not really get to grips with the visual dimension. The use of museum classificatory systems, in which objects may be typologized by function as well as form, goes part of the way towards a workable system, but only part of the way.

To return to the issue of visual research presentation, if the proposed outcome is a fixed or stable text, in the sense that a user is intended neither to add nor subtract from it and to follow a clear line of argument (Fischer and Zeitlyn's 'film' model of multimedia), then the coding of the visual images within it is probably a matter of concern only for the creator as she selects the images and text passages that compose it. If, however, the user is intended to work with the materials in a more analytical fashion, then careful thought needs to be given to the coding and use of meta-data.

Biella et al.'s multimedia reworking of Asch and Chagnon's 1975 Yanomamo film, already discussed above, provides a good example of this (Biella et al., 1997). Although it conforms in one sense to the 'book' model in that there is a core text (the film), the additional materials are far more than footnotes, as there are extensive hyperlinks between all the layers of material. This is in part achieved by creating hyperlinks between images (photographs and film frames) and text, as well as more conventionally between lexical items. For example, clicking on an individual's name in a passage of text can call up other texts referencing the name in other panes of the framed interface, but it can also call up photographs of the individual, a genealogical diagram with the named individual at the centre or, most impressively, successive sequences of the film, where the individual is identified among the often confusing blur of people with a red cross. In order to have achieved this, Biella and associates needed to have added meta-data, including x and y co-ordinates (to indicate the location of the red cross), to dozens if not hundreds of digital film frames.

The emphasis of *Yanomamo Interactive* is very much on the individual people involved, and their kin relations, which is in line with the argument of the original film. Items of material culture are not coded in the same way as that described above; one cannot follow a line of text and images relating the word or item 'ax', for example, still less for abstractions such as 'fight'. Nonetheless, the linking between layers permits a full exploration of the film's original argument (a neo-Darwinian thesis proposing a linkage between degree of kin relatedness and level and types of alliance in aggressive contexts), as well as the exploration of additional lines of inquiry. In one of the essays that comprise the package, Biella suggests that an alternative narrative concerning the role of women in Yanomamo society and the part they may play in settling disputes can be uncovered through judicious use of the hyperlinks, despite the fact that women and their activities are barely mentioned in the original film narration, or highlighted by the camera.

Coding in this way clearly requires an enormous degree of effort, and an extremely thorough knowledge of the research materials, to say nothing of the time taken by design decisions and implementation as documented by Aston (2003). The extraordinary commitment shown by some social researchers producing multimedia versions of their research results means that projects need to be extremely carefully thought through in both intellectual and practical terms (Pink provides several useful pointers: 2001, pp. 168–75; 2006). Given that anyone with little or no social research experience or skill can quickly and easily shoot some videotape, write a few paragraphs of descriptive text, and throw the whole lot up onto a website in a matter of hours, it is all the more important that professional evaluation of the visual and multimedia presentation of research results becomes a matter of course, as discussed earlier in this chapter.

▬▬ Key points

- The relationship between image and text is complex; images may well 'speak for themselves', but researchers need to be sure that they speak in a language that the intended audience understands. Before presenting their own visual research results, researchers could spend some time examining the audience response to similar projects and try to judge what makes for a successful reception.
- Research subjects are generally very pleased to see visual materials concerning them, either during or after the process of research, but researchers should be sensitive to issues of privacy when showing pictures of some subjects to others.
- Constructing multimedia presentations of research, such as websites or CD-ROMs, can be extremely time-consuming, especially when the intended audience may have become accustomed to extremely glossy and professional commercial examples. Researchers who self-author their own material should have as many people as possible to proofread and 'test drive' any such output before officially releasing it.

Further reading

There isn't a great deal written about presenting the results of visual research in conventional written form, such as journal articles, and probably the best way to learn is by studying examples in the leading journals (see the 'Further reading' section at the end of Chapter 1); Harper, however, discusses various narrative modes by which images might be presented in photo essay form. Barbash and Taylor is the most detailed and thorough handbook for film and video production in the social sciences. Pink devotes a chapter to multimedia presentation, while Brown and Peers is an excellent example of a collaborative piece of research based upon photo repatriation; the authors also devote considerable space to their research methodology. Gibbs gives an introduction to the use of computers in analyzing qualitative data in general.

Barbash, I. and Taylor, L. (1997) *Cross-Cultural Filmmaking: A Handbook for Making Documentary and Ethnographic Films and Videos*. Berkeley: University of California Press.

Brown, A., Peers, L. and members of the Kainai Nation (2005) *'Pictures Bring Us Messages'/Sinaakssiiksi aohtsimaahpihkookiyaawa: Photographs and Histories from the Kainai Nation*. Toronto: University of Toronto Press.

Gibbs, G. (2007) *Analyzing Qualitative Data* (Book 6 of *The SAGE Qualitative Research Kit*). London: Sage.

Harper, D. (1987a) 'The visual ethnographic narrative', *Visual Anthropology*, 1: 1–20.

Pink, S. (2006) *The Future of Visual Anthropology: Engaging the Senses*. London: Routledge.

6
Conclusion: images and social research

Chapter objectives
After reading this chapter, you should

- have a brief recap of the themes of the book;
- be able to consider visual methodologies in terms of their distinctiveness and robustness; and
- see that the value of visual methodologies lies in their ability to open up new and previously unconsidered lines of inquiry.

Box 6.1   Visual methods as exploratory strategies

Towards the end of writing this book I had a conversation with a colleague who conducts social research in a more applied field than my own. When I described what I was writing about she was curious that there might be a book's worth of material to cover; within her discipline visual methodologies are largely confined to the video recording of interviews. Recording events with the aim of further analysis – recordings that then become recast as 'data' – is of course a perfectly acceptable use of a visual method, and one that requires some forethought in its execution (see Heath and Hindmarsh, 2002, pp 107–9). It is briefly covered in this book, for example in Chapter 2 where I discuss the way in which such use of video recording has extended the range of conversation analysis.

Moving on in our conversation, I briefly outlined photo-elicitation techniques to my colleague, mentioning their value in situations where a wide social or cultural gap exists between researcher and research subject, and where their use could overcome gaps or misunderstandings in communication. My colleague

(Continued)

(Continued)

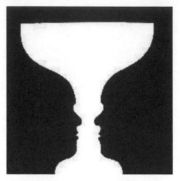

FIGURE 6.1   The 'Rubin vase', an optical illusion normally attributed to
Danish psychologist Edgar Rubin, demonstrating
figure/ground differentiation (see Chapter 1).

suggested work with children as a potential example from her own field and we discussed other social categories of persons where difficulties in linguistic communication might be overcome by using images as a mediator. Again, however, this did not seem to be especially novel methodologically, merely a technical solution to a technical problem.

I then moved on to describe examples where the images raised issues previously unconsidered by social researchers (for example, the work of van der Does and colleagues described in Chapter 4), or where the failure of research subjects to discuss an image could itself be as revealing as their willingness to discuss others (Collier and Collier describe such an instance, related to Navajo anger and hurt over then-US government policy with regard to equestrian stock management: 1986, pp. 112–13).

We were now entering potentially unchartable waters; although there are many examples from the work of other social researchers of the value of employing visual methodologies, these are all subject to post-facto analysis and their findings – by definition – cannot be predicted. They are the 'known unknowns' (to quote Donald Rumsfeld),[41] and while they can be quantified and subject to analysis after their discovery, the problem of the 'unknown unknowns' remains, that is, the things the social researcher did not even know were there to be studied.

My conversation with my colleague continued as I recounted the uses of film or videotape to represent and present to others aspects of human social experience that language cannot fully encompass: the experience a dancer has of her own body, for example, and the way she comprehends the embodied experiences of other dancers. We finished our conversation talking about community and participatory projects, instances such as those described in Chapter 4 where the intellectual aims of the researcher and the social or personal aims of the research subjects coincide.

(Continued)

(Continued)

The initial suppositions of social researchers coming to visual methodologies for the first time are, I think, likely to be rooted in ideas of distinctiveness and robustness. While the first methods my colleague and I discussed – recording data on video-tape and using images to bridge linguistic difficulties in interview contexts – could probably be said to be both distinctive and robust, for many social researchers they would seem to be little more than minor stepping-stones along the research path. The later methods discussed might be novel but are they distinctive, in the sense of yielding sociological insight unrevealed by any other research methodology? And are they robust, in the sense of satisfactorily confirming or repudiating hypotheses in multiple contexts? These questions are addressed in the next sections.

What have we learned?

Over the previous five chapters I have (1) outlined what might be meant by visual methods in social research; (2) described something of the history of these methods in the two principal disciplines that employ them (anthropology and sociology); (3) discussed the various analytical positions formulated with regard to the study and use of images; (4) enumerated a number of methods drawing upon these positions that have been used in fieldwork contexts; and (5) considered the audiences that might read or view the products of visual research and described several modes of research presentation.

Throughout the chapters I have tried to indicate that the development of inter-pretive analytical strategies, including reflexive and collaborative approaches, in the period after the Second World War, and especially since the 1980s, has led to renewed interest in visual research methodologies. Early and perhaps naïve understandings that images automatically encoded evidential truths about social relations were quickly abandoned and replaced with more abstract and quantitative approaches. In recent decades, however, it is clear that such abstractions and quantifications conceal as much as they reveal. In addition, they are rarely comprehensible to the subjects of social research themselves; visual research methods therefore made a comeback in this period. I have also tried to stress that visual research methodologies are of little use in isolation, and in fact it is difficult to see/understand exactly how one would conduct and present social research in a purely visual mode, or at least how it would differ from the social commentary of photo-journalism. Interviews, focus groups, surveys, conversation analysis, all have a valuable and often necessary place in generating qualitative data for sociological insight, not to mention the broad project of ethnographic inquiry that acts as a frame around much if not all field-based research investigation. Very often, the addition of visual methods can bring an added dimension, particularly in realms where the knowledge sought is beyond the range of language. The question is, can visual methodologies yield any new insights beyond those that could be uncovered by other methodological practices? And if so, how robust are these methodologies?

Distinctiveness

Let us consider an example where a research finding is claimed as the unique outcome of the deployment of visual methodology. In the mid-1970s, anthropologist Paul Stoller began conducting field research among the Songhay people of Niger, West Africa, to assess the use of symbolic forms in Songhay local politics (Stoller, 1989). From the outset he was aware that some symbols were straightforwardly visual, and amenable to the most banal visual method of all: simply looking (for example, nobles, the top stratum of the three-part division of society into nobles, former slaves and foreigners, dress in white, signifying that they do not cultivate the soil but pay others to do so; they also carry canes, a symbol of chiefly authority: 1989, p. 57). Stoller, however, claims more substantial insight as a result of his desire to 'see' in the way the Songhay do.

In the course of an exercise to map residences and agricultural land holdings onto the geography of the small town of Mehanna, Stoller noted a correspondence of topographical space and social hierarchy. The fields of the nobles were clustered along the so-called 'Noble' road, while those of their former-slave clients were adjacent to them. The fields of more recently arrived merchants and other migrants were more outlying. Similarly, the residence compounds of the nobles were clustered around the main Friday mosque in the heart of the town (the most sacred space in Songhay society), those of their former-slave clients were again adjacent to them, while those of the foreigners and merchants were most distant from this sacred centre. Again, the method employed, while certainly visual, is not particularly distinctive (I suspect one could have elicited as much simply in conversation) and it is only slightly less banal than observing the symbolic statement made by the colour of the nobles' clothing.

However, Stoller remained troubled by some exceptions to his otherwise neat and static mapping exercise: two merchants had bought fields directly adjacent to the land holdings of the nobles, one former slave had moved his compound from the 'traditional' area to the merchants' residence area, and the wealthiest merchant in the town had moved his compound to the very outskirts of the town, the area normally inhabited by the very poorest of foreigners. Stoller could simply have dismissed these exceptions in the way that quantitative analysts are prone to do – as outliers, or noise in the system, 'data' items of no statistical significance. Instead he sees them as wilful acts; the merchants and the slave had not moved compounds or purchased land accidentally, but neither were their moves purely idiosyncratic. Stoller 'sees' sociological significance in them.

Stoller claims that the introduction of money to Songhay society in the colonial period gradually led to an effective shift of political power from the nobles to the merchants. The merchants, many of whom are also foreigners, are – Stoller claims – aware of this and aware of the symbolic value of their actions. Consequently, some are asserting this new econo-political order by colonizing powerful topographical places in the old order, while others are simply rejecting this old order and reconfiguring space entirely, for example, by establishing a residence on the outskirts of the town. According to Stoller, the merchants and former slaves can 'see' (literally and metaphorically) the changing political order or indeed are actively constituting it topographically and hence visually, while the nobles are 'blinded' by tradition and cannot 'see' what is going on.

Drawing upon the phenomenology of Schutz and Merleau-Ponty, Stoller claims that it was by learning to 'see' in the way that various sections of Songhay society 'see' that he was able to come to this conclusion. Of this I am in no doubt; each social researcher's intellectual journey and hence the methods she deploys along that path are hers alone, and I have no reason to doubt the veracity of Stoller's story. Stoller's account is not explicitly methodological, however, and there is no sure way to know if he could have gained his insight by other means such as interviews and analysis of land title documents. The point, however, is that for this researcher, on this project, a set of visual methods (looking, mapping, learning 'to see') led to a particular finding. Matters of distinctiveness can perhaps only really be settled in tightly controlled, laboratory-like situations, and maybe not even then. Imagine, say, two researchers each directed to interview a group of research subjects to gather evidence to test a hypothesis; unaware of each other's activities, one is supplied with a set of images and instructed in the basics of photo-elicitation, while the other is not. Even if their results were to be dramatically different, there are a number of other variables that might account for the different findings, such as the researchers' general sociological training and their implicit or tacit analytical stance.

Distinctiveness in visual research methodology may be hard to prove conclusively, but it is worth considering the opposite side of the coin: what would social research be like without visual methods? The history of visual methods use described in Chapter 2, the claims for the pervasiveness of visual metaphors and ocularcentrism in contemporary society and the analytical strategies devised to account for them described in Chapter 3, and the various field methods outlined in Chapter 4, would all seem to point to a conclusion that visual methods are both inevitable and necessary. While there are undoubtedly many forms of social research investigation, qualitative as well as quantitative, that do not call for them, there are also forms of investigation that clearly do. Rather than assessing the need, and hence distinctiveness, of visual methods from within the abstractions of sociology, I prefer to see that need and hence distinctiveness as arising from the empirical study of society itself.

117

Robustness

If distinctiveness of visual methods is a slippery concept, at least when viewed from the perspective of more formalist or positivist analytical approaches, then their robustness is probably even more difficult to demonstrate satisfactorily. A statistical procedure when applied to a set of figures will always produce a result; it is a container into which data are placed and which in turn produces a result, another piece of data. Qualitative methodologies do not work in this way, not because the methods are inherently flawed but because the data to which they are applied cannot be neatly brought into sufficient conformity. The quanta or units of qualitative data – interview transcripts, observations, photographs – often share a categorical conformity because the researcher assigns them to categories, not because of a shared ontology.[42] While a researcher could undoubtedly find some form of social organization and behaviour in all societies that she felt happy to label 'marriage' or 'education', it is unlikely that members of all those societies would recognize all the other examples by the same label. Some anthropologists have proposed that even taken-for-granted categories such as 'woman' have little or no analytical validity (e.g. Moore, 1988). Added to this is the problem of meaning, the very problem that many of the formalist analytical strategies discussed in Chapter 3 avoided. A social form such as 'marriage' will mean very different things to people, not only between different societies, but even within a society or section of society.

Some of Stoller's methods described above probably would satisfy a criterion of robustness; procedures for an accurate mapping of topographical space certainly exist, which one could combine with an off-the-shelf procedure for assigning social status to each household head in the town (by income, for example, or by level of social capital). The first part of Stoller's analysis could then be conducted, and the process repeated in other towns and villages in Niger and beyond in order to test some kind of social proximity hypothesis. Unfortunately, Stoller seeks to go beyond this, first by remaining true to an indigenous notion of social stratification (noble, former slave and foreigner), which is therefore difficult to apply to other societies that do not have such a system, and secondly by assuming that research subjects who produce the data are aware of what they are doing and make decisions and choices about their actions, while simultaneously being subject to wider constraints. Through their actions, the subjects generate meaning.

As humans we undoubtedly act for much of the time unconsciously, and in a manner revelatory of wider social forces; this is a sociological fundamental, and lies behind the studies of women's fashion and men's beards discussed in Chapter 3, for example. Yet at the same time we also have agency, are faced with choices, and seek to act to influence others. For much of the time we may do this in sociologically predictable ways – but not always, otherwise there would be no evidence of change in society. And our actions, at least our actions that affect others, are always redolent with meaning; even if we do not intend them as such, then they may be interpreted as such by others. One can perform a series of photo-elicitation exercises over and over with different groups of people and yet the results are never quite the same, because the meanings that people derive from the images – indeed from the research exercise itself – are so varied (Collier and Collier provide numerous examples from their own experience: 1986, chaps 8–10). It is not that the method is necessarily flawed, rather that each instance of human social interaction is always unique. This uniqueness is a quality shared with images themselves: all episodes of *EastEnders* are alike in being examples of the genre soap opera, all photographs of dogs are photographs of dogs. But all are at the same time unique, stubbornly resisting in their creation, consumption and representation the homogenization demanded by robust research methodologies.

Robustness can only be a quality of research methodologies when the messiness of everyday life is smoothed over, decisions made about which features are significant and which can be ignored, and those selected smoothed out into data items, each resembling one another. In a very profound sense, the actual business of living, of conducting social relations, must be conformed to the methodology, rather than vice versa (for an empirical example see Woolgar, 1991). Visual research methodologies, especially those employed in field situations, work against this; whether asking people to talk about images rather than ticking check boxes on a questionnaire, or crafting an ethnographic film rather than writing a research report, visual methods relentlessly particularize, highlight the unique, go beyond the standardization of statistics and language.

On the value of visual methods

My approach above has not been to seek ways in which visual research methodologies can be defended for their distinctive findings, or for the robustness of their operation, in order to lodge them securely in the pantheon of approved methodological approaches in social research. Some methods, particularly those more formalist ones described in Chapter 3, might in fact be defensible in this way. But those approaches depend on a pre-extraction or disembodying of data items from their original empirical context of production in the course of human social relations, just as quantitative methods depend upon a filtering and standardization process to create the supposedly 'raw' data upon which they operate. It is of course the job of sociology and other social research disciplines to do this, to see beyond the individual texture of the bark of trees to the organization of the forest as a whole. But at the same time, there is a risk that abstracted categories such as 'the economy', 'politics', 'social exclusion' and suchlike take on a life of their own; formulated initially as sociological abstractions derived from empirical investigation, they then become reified objects of research in their own right. Meanwhile, ordinary people in society get on with their lives oblivious to these abstractions, wondering whether to plant cash crops to pay school fees and taxes or subsistence crops to feed their families, arguing with their neighbours, grumbling about village elders and corrupt politicians.

The two approaches are not irreconcilable. A humanistic concern with the specificities and fine texture of life-as-it-is-lived can be found in investigative journalism, in the activities of community development activists and in a whole host of other areas. Social research depends crucially upon broader insights derived from social theory, indeed upon abstractions. What visual research methodologies bring to this is a seemingly paradoxical mixing of the singular and the multiple. Singular, because each image when held against the abstraction demands that the general reveal itself in the specific. What is the basis of 'class' as an analytical category if it cannot be seen in any image? Verging towards the more concrete, by what criteria can the category of 'marriage' be imputed to an image of a man and woman standing together? I am not suggesting that either 'class' or 'marriage' are sociologically meaningless abstractions simply because images of them either do not exist, or that an image that some viewers would recognize as being 'of' a marriage would not be recognized by all viewers. What I am suggesting is that the particularity of images – photomechanical images for the most part, but all images by virtue of their singular materiality – can and should provoke the researcher into (re)considering taken-for-granted analytical categories.

Paradoxically, precisely because images can sustain multiple readings, depending on the viewer's social and personal context, they permit multiple forms of analysis. Consequently, the value of visual methodologies lies in promoting exploration, serendipity and social collaboration in social research. Throughout this book, but especially in Chapter 4, I have outlined a number of cases where either a visual methodology is stumbled upon or discovered by a social researcher, or where the visually based research has yielded directions of inquiry previously unconsidered by the researcher, or where the researcher as a member of society has sought to align her research aims with the social concerns of those normally rendered mute and passive as 'research subjects'.

Practitioners of visual methods, when these are skilfully and knowingly deployed, are well aware that the potential limitations of method can easily be turned around to become strengths. Ultimately, the distinctiveness and robustness of visual methods, and consequently what we can learn from them, is not their exclusive insights, nor their verifiability in multiple contexts, but the fact that they are constantly labile, constantly leading research in new directions in a way that matches the fluidity and flux of human experience itself.

▆▆▆ Key points

- Visual research methods can be both distinctive and robust, but their major strength lies in uncovering the previously unknown or unconsidered dimensions of social life; researchers using them should be prepared for the unexpected.
- The aim of this book has been to set researchers on a journey into what is, I hope, a new and exciting terrain, during which they may learn as much about themselves as they do about the research subjects.

‖ Notes

Chapter 1

1 A note on terms and limitations: although I am a social anthropologist by training, I have tried as hard as possible to make the discussion in this and subsequent chapters relevant to researchers across a broad range of social science disciplines. I have therefore adopted the rather bland terms 'social research' and 'social researcher', though I recognize that there is no such thing as a generic social researcher. The reader will therefore have to ask herself how what I am discussing might be made most relevant to a psychological study, or a political science study, and so forth. I also use the term 'sociological' as a catch-all term to cover the insights gained from any kind of social research. Similarly, although in this and subsequent chapters I will be talking about 'pictures' and 'images', I generally have in mind photographs and, to some extent, film or videotape. Again, the particular medium used for image creation and dissemination is important, and the researcher should also be asking herself whether what I say about photography, for example, also applies to painting, or sand drawing, or whatever. Finally, I adopt the admittedly depersonalizing term 'research subjects' to indicate the men and women (and children) from whom fieldworking social researchers gather data. Particular disciplines may customarily use generalizing terms such as 'informants' or 'respondents', and particular authors may avoid all such terms and instead specify through description ('a neighbour') or pseudonym ('Jane'). My use of 'research subjects' is intended to cover all of these without prejudice.

2 In the wake of George W. Bush's declaration of a 'war' on terror, and the consequent tightening of security at airports in the US and elsewhere, research into biometric identification systems is on the increase. While iris scanning seems relatively well developed, the far less intrusive computer comparison of faces with photographs is not currently well advanced. Variations in lighting and posture, and changes due to age, illness or cosmetic surgery, all serve to introduce too much variation.

Chapter 2

3 This is a hugely superficial summary of only one part of the Victorian anthropological project. For critical overviews of the (spurious) notion of there being a social evolutionary progression from 'primitive' to 'civilized' society, see Fabian (1983), Kuper (1988) and Stocking (1982). Edwards (1992, 2001) provides more information on the role of photography in these projects.

4 The quotations from the FSA shooting scripts are taken from appendixes to a longer, unpublished version of Suchar's paper, given as a presentation to an International Visual Studies Association meeting in 1989 (see Flaes, 1989). More information on the

FSA photographic work can be found in Trachtenberg (1989), while Collier and Collier's early work on visual research methods (1986, originally 1967) grew out of John Collier's work for the FSA in the 1940s.

5   Although I will mention his work in passing elsewhere in this book, this is not the place to discuss the enormous influence David MacDougall has had on the history of post-1960s ethnographic film, both through his own films (often jointly with Judith MacDougall) and through his writing on film and visual anthropology. See Grimshaw (2001) and Loizos (1993) for appraisals, as well as MacDougall (1998) for some of his essays.

6   Briefly, and anticipating the discussion of Chapter 3, I am therefore excluding firstly the many studies of advertising and other images that are consumed within Euro-American society. This is on the grounds that such studies pay scant attention to the human agents involved in the production of such images, generally ascribing them to 'society' in a rather vague sense; that is, 'society' somehow produces images that employ codes that Euro-Americans read or that reflect Euro-American 'society's' norms or values. Such studies therefore begin the work of sociological analysis at far too late a point in the process, however valuable the subsequent semiotic analysis may be. Secondly, I exclude the literature from design that discusses the 'best' way to present visual material – again, largely and unquestioningly oriented towards an essentially a-historical Euro-American understanding of society. This literature is both interesting and valuable for those involved in the relevant industries, but again, it does not strike me as especially sociological, except in the presumptions made.

Chapter 3

7   Jenkins makes these remarks in praise of the sociologist Pierre Bourdieu's skill in this area, but achieving a productive dialogue between 'theory' and practice is a goal for all anthropologists.

8   In order for me to be able to formulate some of these statements, it should, I hope, be obvious that I situate myself within a broadly interpretivist and reflexive paradigm. That is, my personal epistemology contains within it the apparent ability to think both within the paradigm and at the same time to stand outside it and consider both it and the other major paradigm. While admittedly paradoxical, there is not very much I can do about this! All I can say is that I hope I can present the various perspectives discussed in the text in as fair a fashion as possible.

9   Of course, there are entire disciplines wholly concerned with image analysis, most notably art history and film studies. Although there are important exceptions, these disciplines have not historically been overly concerned with social issues, nor have they taken a distinctively sociological approach to the study of visual images. I do not discuss them further here.

10   I have of necessity to be selective in what is covered in this section. Perhaps the most significant omission is a sustained discussion of psychoanalytical approaches; Gillian Rose provides an admirable summary (2001, chap. 5).

11   I have expanded imaginatively on Lister and Wells's discussion of the image.

12   I am well aware of the irony of making this statement and indeed providing this example in a book intended for use on research methods courses.

13   Strictly, Haddon was of course studying the things – baskets, pots, or whatever – rather than images as such. For *Evolution in Art* he examined objects in a variety of museums, as well as drawings and photographs made by others. The point seems banal, but is typical of the slipperiness and elisions that exist between things and images of things in much analysis.

14   The underlying theoretical influence implied appears to be a form of Durkheimian functionalism; see Besnard (1994) for a recent, non-visual and more explicitly Durkheimian example, and see of course Durkheim's *Suicide* (1951).

15   Heath and Hindmarsh also provide an outline of an extended transcription system for annotating the video material.

16   At a more abstract level, Giddens (1991) uses the term to indicate the constant process of self-examination and refashioning that modernity demands of society's members . This macro-perspective can be understood as a context for the more narrowly methodologically practical discussion of the term here.

17   Key works normally associated with identifying (or, some would say, creating) this 'crisis' are Clifford and Marcus (1986), Marcus and Fischer (1986), Marcus and Cushman (1982) and Clifford (1988). From these, especially various contributions in the first volume, there spiralled out a vast literature.

18   Regardless of underlying theoretical presumptions it is, I think, possible to discuss 'good' and 'bad' applications of method or analysis; that is, some projects are simply poorly conceived and poorly conducted. While the standards by which projects are measured are in part set by the framing theoretical paradigm (for example, within a quantitative, positivist paradigm, the failure to distinguish between a 'random' dataset of images selected to investigate, say, gender inequality in advertising, and an 'opportunistic' dataset is a serious flaw), I think it is possible to identify some universal weaknesses that any social scientist, no matter what their theoretical persuasion, would regard as compromising to the project. Chief amongst these would be the elevation, usually implicit, of a researcher's opinion (on, for example, what a photograph 'means') to the level of a 'truth' that is valid for all members of their society and, indeed, for humankind universally. This kind of flaw is more common than might be imagined, and is often concealed by bombastic or supposedly 'difficult' prose.

Chapter 4

19   Many of the examples described in this chapter and the next are drawn from my earlier book on visual methods (Banks, 2001), although often recast to suit the agenda of this volume.

20   By 'the field' I merely mean any real-world context in which people are going about their daily business and into which the researcher aims to insert herself for a shorter or longer duration, in contrast to the library or office, or the experimental laboratory.

21   The anthropologist Janet Hoskins (1998) considers the reverse situation, where a discussion of objects can help illuminate the biographies of people.

22   As an aside, some teachers of both film and visual anthropology occasionally set a training exercise for students in which a 'picture off' button would be very useful. A sequence of film without sound is played to a class, followed by a soundtrack with no accompanying picture. The students are asked to describe what they understand: where in the world are we? what are they doing? how might soundtrack help to structure the images? what kind of pictures might accompany these sounds? and so on. However, the point of this exercise is not so much to conduct any kind of experiment with the students, but rather to use it as the starting point for developing their visual literacy, helping them to make explicit and self-conscious their tacit film reading skills (see also Martinez, 1990, p. 46).

23   Barbash and Taylor's comprehensive *Cross-Cultural Filmmaking* (1997) is valuable for far more than strictly ethnographic film production, and covers a huge range of technical issues as well as more general discussions of film styles, ethics, and so forth (see also Asch, 1992). Nothing quite equivalent exists for either still photography or video (though some useful insights are to be found in Wright, 1999, for the former and Harding, 1997, for the latter). Sarah Pink's *Doing Visual Ethnography* (2001) contains two chapters on the use of photography and the use of video in ethnographic fieldwork, which while not strictly technical do make a number of practical points.

24 Some commentators (e.g. Ruby, 2005, p. 112) understand the ciné-trance idea to mean that the subjects of the film (rather than the filmmaker) enter into a trance-like state and in doing so reveal themselves and their culture to the camera in a way that would not be possible by other means. It is entirely possible that Rouch used the idea in both ways, and it is certainly in accordance with the idea discussed in the section about collaboration in this chapter that the very fact of engaging with social research causes research subjects to reflect on themselves and their social position.

25 Almost every anthropologist from Euro-America who has worked in the developing world has worked with people who have expectations, some realistic, some not, of what the anthropologist may be able to do for them: providing jobs overseas, intervening with local officials, acting as a channel for aid projects or tourist ventures, and so forth.

26 Chalfen's introduction to the second edition of the book (originally published in 1972) summarizes the responses to the project (Chalfen, 1996).

27 I should quickly say that I have no problem with advocacy projects conducted by social researchers. My point here is merely to create a category distinction between visual projects commissioned by a group of research subjects for their own ends in which the researcher is essentially a facilitator, and those in which the political or social goals of the group are matched by a disciplinary, rather than an ethical or political, interest on the part of the researcher. The distinction is, I admit, a fine one.

28 This is most easily accessed online at www.theasa.org.

29 Some anthropologists have found to their cost that this may not be sufficient. In groups that have a strong sense of collective identity, the fact that the identity of specific individuals is concealed is irrelevant. If an anonymized individual is described as doing something shameful, illegal, or merely embarrassing, the group as a whole (or leaders claiming to speak on behalf of the group as a whole) may take offence at the circulation of the representation.

30 I am not a lawyer and my understanding of these issues is at a very superficial level. Social researchers who think they have good reason to be concerned about such matters should consult a media lawyer or any other lawyer practiced in these issues. My understanding, however, is that there are many grey areas and few clear-cut answers.

31 That the subjects of images have no automatic legal entitlement to copyright in those images was shown in 1998, when the Diana, Princess of Wales, Memorial Fund sought legal action against a North American manufacturer of commemorative items claiming that a 'Diana' doll it was producing 'exploited' the late woman's identity (*Electronic Telegraph*, issue 1089, 19 May 1998); a year earlier the Memorial Fund had sought to register Diana's image as a trademark. Both actions failed.

Chapter 5

32 That said, there are many social science departments in the UK – including my own at doctoral level – that would not accept a film (for example) as an inherent part of a dissertation's argument, but only as an annexe to a written dissertation that the examiners would not necessarily be obliged to view.

33 One could also argue the contrary position, that photographs are and remain too powerful in their representational properties to be constrained in this way.

34 I regard the first 'audience' as somewhat self-evident and it is disingenuous to pretend otherwise.

35 'Research footage' is of course another matter; when a social researcher has shot film or videotape as part of a data-gathering exercise it is likely she will form the sole audience, certainly for the entirety of the material, though extracts may be screened in the course of conference presentations.

36 Ironically, perhaps, Bell had not at the time of publication deposited copies of the images he took to the Purari Delta as local storage conditions are not yet sufficient to preserve paper in the humid climate, though this is planned (J. Bell, 2003, p. 119). But he is quite clear – as am I – that he repatriated the idea or meaning of the images and that within the local cultural context the oral and material discourse surrounding the images is more important than the photographic objects themselves.

37 In the course of his article, Geffroy – who has psychoanalytical training – does in fact make some psychoanalytical readings of the villagers' photographs, especially regarding gender and marital relationships.

38 Quality can in fact be diminished if 'lossy' compression formats such as JPEG are used, which drop supposedly redundant pixels; TIFF is a preferred format for image files. Equally, scanning (or still digital photograph creation) should be done at the highest possible resolution, regardless of file size. Resolution can be diminished, for example to create small files for electronic transmission, but it can never be augmented. Electronic file storage is now so cheap and computer processing power now so great that the huge file sizes of high-resolution TIFF images are not the obstacle that they once were.

39 The Uduk people have been refugees since the late 1980s, forced to cross the border between Sudan and Ethiopia a number of times. James's recent work has documented the upheavals in their lives, a corpus that includes both the television film (*Orphans of Passage*, MacDonald, 1993) and the journal article upon which this multi-media project is based (James, 1997). The multimedia project itself was devised as a kind of annexe to an earlier large-scale project, 'Experience-Rich Anthropology' (ERA), which sought to create multimedia texts based on the work of a variety of anthropologists, which could be used in teaching the discipline. The ERA projects, coordinated by Michael Fischer and David Zeitlyn, can be found online at era.anthropology.ac.uk.

40 A full discussion of manual and computer-based coding systems for text is well beyond the scope of this book; see J. Fielding (2001) and Gibbs (2007) for good introductions.

Chapter 6

41 In 2002 the then US Secretary of Defense Donald Rumsfeld commented on the likelihood of linkages between Saddam Hussein's regime in Baghdad and terrorist organizations such as al-Qaeda by referrring to the 'known knowns', the 'known unknowns' and the 'unknown unknowns'; this gnomic statement was subsequently rendered into poetry form by Seely (2003). In many ways, visual research methodologies provide access into not just the 'known unknowns' but also the 'unknown unknowns'.

42 Where this is less true is when language, or more particularly linguistic analysis, is involved. Because at the level of *langue* and perhaps at the level of *parole* language does exhibit regularities and rule-governed behaviour, it is possible to assign categories for analysis and to standardize and regularize lexical items as data. This process may, however, overlook the ways in which language is put to social use, such as irony.

||| Glossary

Agency The ability of a person or group to exercise social action (see also Chapter 1).

Anthropometry The measurement of the human body; anthropometric photography seeks to capture data about body shape and type in a standardized form.

Choreometrics A system, devised by Alan Lomax, to analyze dance movement cross-culturally.

Conversation analysis The study of language use in specific real-world situations; increasingly, film and videotaped recordings of conversational encounters allow consideration of gesture as well.

Data A datum (singular) is a discrete item selected or created for analysis, such as a set of figures or an instance of behaviour (see also Chapter 1).

Documentary With regard to film, generally covering all non-fiction film that has a narrative (as opposed to, say, a newsreel) (see also Chapter 1).

Ethnographic film A **documentary** film genre seeking to portray (some part of) the life of a society or social group.

Ethnography The on-the-ground qualitative study of the life of a society or social group, typically through **participant-observation** (see also Box 4.1 in Chapter 4).

Ethnology A now largely discarded term indicating the **ethnographic** study of a society, or often, the comparison of a feature or features across several societies.

Fieldwork A broad term indicating the researcher's presence among the research subjects in their normal environment of social interaction; the researcher will use a variety of methods during fieldwork (see also Box 4.1 in Chapter 4).

Figure/ground Along with **perspective** and **representation**, this is one of a number of terms taken from the visual arts to draw attention to the viewer and their engagement with an image; in this case, how the key elements of a composition are related to the embedding context (see also Chapter 1).

Frame Literally, the frame around an image (or a single image in a sequence, such as in a film strip), but also the intellectual questions that delineate the parameters of a piece of research (see also Chapter 1).

Frame-still A still image extracted from a sequence of moving images and reproduced, for example as an illustration in a book.

Jump-cut A form of film or video editing where two scenes of similar content are edited together such that the action appears to jump rather than flow smoothly.

Latent The underlying meaning of something (a statement, an image, etc.) rather than the apparently obvious, or **manifest**, meaning.

Manifest The on-the-surface appearance of something, or the intended meaning of something; see also **latent**.

Materiality A term to draw attention to the social significance of the material properties of things.

Metadata Data about **data**; if an object or image is understood as an item of data, then the description of the item constitutes its metadata; metadata are typically far more structured and regular than the data items they describe and hence allow more systematic analysis.

Multivocality See **polyvocality**.

Narrative Briefly, the 'story' told by a sequence of words, actions or images, and more generally the organization of the information within that story (see also Chapter 1).

Ocularcentrism A term to denote the apparent centrality of vision in the modern world's understanding of itself (see also Chapter 1).

Participant-observation A fieldwork method used by anthropologists and others where the researcher seeks as far as possible to participate in the social life of the research subjects, as well as – paradoxically – standing apart from that social life in order to observe it.

Perspective An interest in perspective in the technical sense encourages visual research to pay more attention to the location and viewpoint of the observer (see also Chapter 1).

Polyvocality The 'many voices' with which images may speak, that is, the different meanings that can be attributed to an image by different observers.

Proxemics The study of the (social) use of space and what is sometimes called 'personal territory'; as with **choreometrics**, film and videotape are often used to capture data for subsequent analysis.

Reflexivity The process by which a researcher considers and accounts for their own role in the conduct of research and analysis of the findings (see also Chapter 1).

Representation One thing (a verbal utterance, a picture, etc.) standing for another thing (an act witnessed, a person) but not identical to it; the representation is a thing-in-itself, not just a substitute for something else (see also Chapter 1).

Scopic regime A form of social control or order which rests primarily upon vision – the act of seeing and the condition of being seen – to maintain that order.

Semiotic analysis The study of signs or symbols, particularly systems of linked signs, and how meaning is communicated in predictable and structured ways by them.

III References

Abu-Lughod, L. (1995) 'The objects of soap opera: Egyptian television and the cultural politics of modernity', in D. Miller (ed.), *Worlds Apart: Modernity Through the Prism of the Local*. London: Routledge, pp. 190–210.

Alexander, V. (2001) 'Analysing visual materials', in N. Gilbert (ed.), *Researching Social Life*. London: Sage, pp. 343–57.

Angrosino, M. (2007) *Doing Ethnographic and Observational Research* (Book 3 of *The SAGE Qualitative Research Kit*). London: Sage.

Appadurai, A. (ed.) (1986) *The Social Life of Things: Commodities in Cultural Perspective*. Cambridge: Cambridge University Press.

Asch, T. (1992) 'The ethics of ethnographic film-making', in P.I. Crawford and D. Turton (eds), *Film as Ethnography*. Manchester: Manchester University Press, pp. 196–204.

Asch, P. and Connor, L. (1994) 'Opportunities for "double-voicing" in ethnographic film', *Visual Anthropology Review*, 10: 14–27.

Aston, J. (2003) 'Interactive multimedia: an investigation into its potential for communicating ideas and arguments', PhD thesis, Royal College of Art and University of Cambridge, London and Cambridge.

Aufderheide, P. (1995) 'The Video in the Villages project: videomaking with and by Brazilian Indians', *Visual Anthropology Review*, 11: 83–93.

Ball, M. (1998) 'Remarks on visual competence as an integral part of ethnographic fieldwork practice: the visual availability of culture', in J. Prosser (ed.), *Image-Based Research: A Sourcebook for Qualitative Researchers*. London: Falmer Press, pp. 131–47.

Ball, M. and Smith, G.W.H. (1992) *Analyzing Visual Data*. London: Sage.

Banks, M. (1996) 'Constructing the audience through ethnography', in P.I. Crawford and S.B. Hafsteinsson (eds), *The Construction of the Viewer: Proceedings from NAFA 3*. Højbjerg, Denmark: Intervention Press, pp. 118–34.

Banks, M. (2001) *Visual Methods in Social Research*. London: Sage.

Barbash, I. and Taylor, L. (1997) *Cross-Cultural Filmmaking: A Handbook for Making Documentary and Ethnographic Films and Videos*. Berkeley: University of California Press.

Barbour, R. (2007) *Doing Focus Groups* (Book 4 of *The SAGE Qualitative Research Kit*). London: Sage.

Barnouw, E. (1983) *Documentary: A History of the Non-fiction Film* (rev. ed.). Oxford: Oxford University Press.

Barry, A. (1995) 'Reporting and visualising', in C. Jenks (ed.), *Visual Culture*. London: Routledge, pp. 42–57.

Barthes, R. (1973) *Mythologies*. London: Paladin.

Bateson, G. and Mead, M. (1942) *Balinese Character: A Photographic Analysis*. New York: New York Academy of Sciences.

Becker, H. (1982) *Art Worlds*. Berkeley: University of California Press.

References

Becker, H. (1998) *Tricks of the Trade: How to Think About Your Research While You're Doing it*. Chicago: University of Chicago Press.

Becker, H. and Hagaman, D. (2003) 'Afterword: digital image ethics', in L. Gross, J. Katz and J. Ruby (eds), *Image Ethics in the Digital Age*. Minneapolis: University of Minnesota Press, pp. 343–9.

Becker, H.S. (1974) 'Photography and sociology', *Studies in the Anthropology of Visual Communication* 1, 3–26. Republished in H.S. Becker (1986) *Doing Things Together: Selected Papers*. Evanston: Northwestern University Press; also available online at lucy.ukc.ac.uk/becker.html.

Bell, J. (2003) 'Looking to see: reflections on visual repatriation in the Purari Delta, Gulf Province, Papua New Guinea', in L. Peers and A. Brown (eds), *Museums and Source Communities: A Routledge Reader*. London: Routledge, pp. 111–22.

Bell, P. (2001) 'Content analysis of visual images', in T. van Leeuwen and C. Jewitt (eds), *Handbook of Visual Analysis*. London: Sage, pp. 10–34.

Berelson, B. (1952) *Content Analysis in Communication Research*. New York: Free Press.

Berger, J. (1972) *Ways of Seeing*. London: BBC/Penguin.

Berger, J. and Mohr, J. (1967) *A Fortunate Man: The Story of a Country Doctor*. Harmondsworth: Allen Lane/Penguin.

Berger, J. and Mohr, J. (1975) *A Seventh Man: A Book of Images and Words About the Experience of Migrant Workers in Europe*. Harmondsworth: Penguin.

Berger, J. and Mohr, J. (1982) *Another Way of Telling*. London: Writers and Readers.

Besnard, P. (1994) 'A Durkheimian approach to the study of fashion: the sociology of Christian or first names', in W.S.F. Pickering and H. Martins (eds), *Debating Durkheim*. London: Routledge, in conjunction with the British Centre for Durkheimian Studies, pp. 159–73.

Biella, P., Chagnon, N.A. and Seaman, G. (1997) *Yanomamo Interactive: The Ax Fight*. New York: Harcourt Brace.

Biella, P. (1988) 'Against reductionism and idealist self-reflexivity: the Ilparakuyo Maasai film project', in J. Rollwagon (ed.), *Anthropological Filmmaking: Anthropological Perspectives on the Production of Film and Video for the General Public* Chur: Harwood Academic Press, pp. 47–73.

Brown, A., Peers, L. and members of the Kainai Nation (2005) 'Pictures Bring Us Messages/ Sinaakssiiksi aohtsimaahpihkookiyaawa: Photographs and Histories from the Kainai Nation*. Toronto: University of Toronto Press.

Caldarola, V. (1985) 'Visual contexts: a photographic research method in anthropology', *Studies in Visual Communication,* 11: 33–53.

Carelli, V. (1988) 'Vidéo dans les villages: un instrument de réaffirmation ethnique', *CVA Newsletter*, October: 13–19.

Chalfen, R. (1996) 'Foreword', in S. Worth and J. Adair (eds), *Through Navajo Eyes: An Exploration in Film Communication and Anthropology*. Albuquerque: University of New Mexico Press, pp. ix–xxii.

Chaplin, E. (1994) *Sociology and Visual Representation*. London: Routledge.

Chaplin, E. (1998) 'Making meanings in art worlds: a sociological account of the career of John Constable and his oeuvre, with special reference to "The Cornfield" (homage to Howard Becker)', in J. Prosser (ed.), *Image-Based Research: A Sourcebook for Qualitative Researchers*. London: Falmer Press, pp. 284–306.

Chiozzi, P. (1989) 'Photography and anthropological research: three case studies', in R. Boonzajer Flaes (ed.), *Eyes Across the Water: The Amsterdam Conference on Visual Anthropology and Sociology*. Amsterdam: Het Spinhuis, pp. 43–50.

Clifford, J. (1988) *The Predicament of Culture: Twentieth Century Ethnography, Literature and Art*. Cambridge, MA: Harvard University Press.

References

Clifford, J. and Marcus, G.E. (1986) *Writing Culture: The Poetics and Politics of Ethnography.* Berkeley: University of California Press.

Collier, J. and Collier, M. (1986) *Visual Anthropology: Photography as a Research Method.* Albuquerque: University of New Mexico Press.

Coover, R. (2004a) 'Using digital media tools in cross-cultural research, analysis and representation', *Visual Studies,* 19: 6–25.

Coover, R. (2004b) 'Working with images, images of work: using digital interface, photography and hypertext in ethnography', in S. Pink, L. Kürti and A.I. Afonso (eds), *Working Images: Visual Research and Representation in Ethnography,* London: Routledge, pp. 185–203.

Cronin, Ó. (1998) 'Psychology and photographic theory', in J. Prosser (ed.), *Image-Based Research: A Sourcebook for Qualitative Researchers.* London: Falmer Press, pp. 69–83.

Danforth, L. and Tsiaras, A. (1982) *The Death Rituals of Rural Greece.* Princeton: Princeton University Press.

Darvin, C. (1872) *The Expression of the Emotions in Man and Animals.* London: John Murry.

Davis, J. (1989) 'The social relations of the production of history', in E. Tonkin, M. McDonald and M. Chapman (eds), *History and Ethnicity.* London: Routledge, pp. 104–20.

de Brigard, E. (1995 (1975)) 'The history of ethnographic film', in P. Hockings (ed.), *Principles of Visual Anthropology* (2nd edn). The Hague: Mouton, pp. 13–43.

de Laine, M. (2000). *Fieldwork, Participation and Practice: Ethics and Dilemmas in Qualitative Research.* London: Sage.

Diem-Wille, G. (2001) 'A therapuetic perspective: the use of drawings in child psychoanalysis and social science', in T. van Leeuwen and C. Jewitt (eds), *Handbook of Visual Analysis.* London: Sage, pp. 119–33.

Dowmunt, T. (ed.) (1993) *Channels of Resistance: Global Television and Local Empowerment.* London: BFI Publishing, in association with Channel Four Television.

Dresch, P., James, W. and Parkin, D. (eds) (2000) *Anthropologists in a Wider World: Essays on Field Research.* Oxford: Berghahn Books.

Durkheim, E. (1951) *Suicide.* Glencoe, IL: The Free Press.

Eaton, M. (1979) 'The production of cinematic reality', in M. Eaton (ed.), *Anthropology-Reality-Cinema: The Films of Jean Rouch.* London: British Film Institute, pp. 40–53.

Edgar, I. (2004) 'Imagework in ethnographic research', in S. Pink, L. Kürti and A.I. Afonso (eds), *Working Images: Visual Research and Representation in Ethnography.* London: Routledge, pp. 90–106.

Edwards, E. (ed.) (1992) *Anthropology and Photography 1860–1920.* New Haven: Yale University Press, in association with The Royal Anthropological Institute, London.

Edwards, E. (2001) *Raw Histories: Photographs, Anthropology and Museums.* Oxford: Berg.

Edwards, E. (2003) 'Talking visual histories: introduction', in L. Peers and A. Brown (eds), *Museums and Source Communities: A Routledge Reader.* London: Routledge, pp. 83–99.

Ellen, R.F. (ed.) (1984) *Ethnographic Research: A Guide to General Conduct.* London: Academic Press.

Emmison, M. and Smith, P. (2000) *Researching the Visual: Images, Objects, Contexts and Interactions in Social and Cultural Enquiry.* London: Sage.

Evans, J. and Hall, S. (1999) 'What is visual culture?', in J. Evans and S. Hall (eds), *Visual Culture: The Reader.* London: Sage, in association with the Open University.

Fabian, J. (1983) *Time and the Other: How Anthropology Makes Its Object.* New York: Columbia University Press.

Faris, J.C. (1992) 'Anthropological transparency: film, representation and politics', in P. Crawford and D. Turton (eds), *Film as Ethnography.* Manchester: Manchester University Press, in association with the Granada Centre for Visual Anthropology, pp. 171–82.

Faris, J.C. (1993) 'A response to Terence Turner', *Anthropology Today,* 9: 12–13.

References

Fielding, J. (2001) 'Coding and managing data', in N. Gilbert (ed.), *Researching Social Life*. London: Sage, pp. 227–51.

Fielding, N. (2001) 'Ethnography', in N. Gilbert (ed.), *Researching Social Life*. London: Sage, pp. 145–63.

Fischer, M.D. and Zeitlyn, D. (2003) 'Visual anthropology in the digital mirror: computer-assisted visual anthropology'. Canterbury: Centre for Social Anthropology and Computing, http://lucy.ukc.ac.uk/dz/layers_nggwun.html

Flaes, R.B. (ed.) (1989) *Eyes Across the Water: The Amsterdam Conference on Visual Anthropology and Sociology*. Amsterdam: Het Spinhuis.

Flick, U. (2007a) *Designing Qualitative Research* (Book 1 of *The SAGE Qualitative Research Kit*). London: Sage.

Flick, U. (2007b) *Managing Quality in Qualitative Research* (Book 8 of *The SAGE Qualitative Research Kit*). London: Sage.

Foucault, M. (1973) *The Birth of the Clinic: An Archeology of Medical Perception*. London: Tavistock.

Foucault, M. (1977) *Discipline and Punish: The Birth of the Prison*. London: Allen Lane.

Geertz, C. (1973) 'Deep play. Notes on the Balinese cock-fight', in *The Interpretation of Cultures*. New York: Basic Books, pp. 412–53.

Geffroy, Y. (1990) 'Family photographs: a visual heritage', *Visual Anthropology*, 3: 367–410.

Gell, A. (1992) 'The technology of enchantment and the enchantment of technology', in J. Coote and A. Shelton (eds), *Anthropology, Art and Aesthetics* (Oxford Studies in the Anthropology of Cultural Forms). Oxford: Clarendon Press, pp. 40–63.

Gell, A. (1998) *Art and Agency: An Anthropological Theory*. Oxford: Clarendon.

Gibbs, G. (2007) *Analyzing Qualitative Data* (Book 6 of *The SAGE Qualitative Research Kit*). London: Sage.

Giddens, A. (1991) *Modernity and Self-Identity*. Cambridge: Polity.

Ginsburg, F. (1991) 'Indigenous media: Faustian contract or global village?', *Cultural Anthropology*, 6: 92–112.

Ginsburg, F. (1994) 'Culture/media: a (mild) polemic', *Anthropology Today*, 10: 5–15.

Ginsburg, F. (1999) 'The parallax effect: the impact of indigenous media on ethnographic film', in J.M. Gaines and M. Renov (eds), *Collecting Visible Evidence*. Minneapolis: University of Minnesota Press, pp. 156–75.

Glaser, B.G. and Strauss, A.L. (1967) *The Discovery of Grounded Theory: Strategies for Qualitative Research*. New York: Aldine.

Gold, S. (1991) 'Ethnic boundaries and ethnic entrepreneurship: a photo-elicitation study', *Visual Sociology*, 6(2): 9–22.

Goodwin, C. (2001) 'Practices of seeing visual analysis: an ethnomethodological approach', in T. van Leeuwen and C. Jewitt (eds), *Handbook of Visual Analysis*. London: Sage, pp. 157–182.

Gould, S.J. (1981) *The Mismeasure of Man*. New York: W.W. Norton.

Grady, J. (1991) 'The visual essay and sociology', *Visual Sociology*, 6: 23–38.

Griffiths, A. (2002) *Wondrous Difference: Cinema, Anthropology and Turn-of-the-Century Visual Culture*. New York: Columbia University Press.

Grimshaw, A. (2001) *The Ethnographer's Eye: Ways of Seeing in Anthropology*. Cambridge: Cambridge University Press.

Gross, L., Katz, J. and Ruby, J. (eds) (1988) *Image Ethics: The Moral Rights of Subjects in Photographs, Film, and Television*. New York; Oxford: Oxford University Press.

Gross, L., Katz, J. and Ruby, J. (eds) (2003) *Image Ethics in the Digital Age*. Minneapolis: University of Minnesota Press.

Gupta, A. and Ferguson, J. (1992) 'Beyond "Culture": space, identity, and the politics of difference', *Cultural Anthropology*, 7: 6–23.

References

Haddon, A.C. (1895) *Evolution in Art: As Illustrated by the Life-Histories of Designs*. London: Walter Scott.

Halpern, S.W. (2003) 'Copyright law and the challenge of digital technology', in L. Gross, J. Katz and J. Ruby (eds), *Image Ethics in the Digital Age*. Minneapolis: University of Minnesota Press, pp. 143–70.

Hammersley, M. and Atkinson, P. (1983). *Ethnography: Principles in Practice*. London: Tavistock.

Hamilton, P. and Hargreaves, R. (2001) *The Beautiful and the Dammed: The Creation of Identity in Nineteenth-Century Portrait Photography*. London: National Portrait Gallery.

Harding, T. (1997) *The Video Activist Handbook*. London: Pluto.

Harper, D. (1982) *Good Company*. Chicago: University of Chicago Press.

Harper, D. (1987a) 'The visual ethnographic narrative', *Visual Anthropology*, 1: 1–20.

Harper, D. (1987b) *Working Knowledge: Skill and Community in a Small Shop*. Chicago: University of Chicago Press.

Harper, D. (1989) 'Visual sociology: expanding the sociological vision', in G. Blank, J. McCartney and E. Brent (eds), *New Technology in Sociology*. New Brunswick, NJ: Transaction Publishers, pp. 81–97.

Harper, D. (1998) 'An argument for visual sociology', in J. Prosser (ed.), *Image-Based Research: A Sourcebook for Qualitative Researchers*. London: Falmer Press, pp. 24–41.

Heath, C. and Hindmarsh, J. (2002) 'Analysing interaction: video, ethnography and situated conduct', in T. May (ed.), *Qualitative Research in Action*. London: Sage, pp. 99–121.

Heider, K. (1976) *Ethnographic Film*. Austin: University of Texas Press.

Henley, P. (2004) 'Putting film to work: observational cinema as practical ethnography', in S. Pink, L. Kürti and A.I. Afonso (eds), *Working Images: Visual Research and Representation in Ethnography*. London: Routledge, pp. 109–30.

Herle, A. and Rouse, S. (eds) (1998) *Cambridge and the Torres Strait: Centenary Essays on the 1898 Anthropological Expedition*. Cambridge: Cambridge University Press.

Hoskins, J. (1998) *Biographical Objects: How Things Tell the Stories of People's Lives*. New York: Routledge.

Iedema, R. (2001) 'Analysing film and television: a social semiotic account of *Hospital*: an unhealthy business', in T. van Leeuwen and C. Jewitt (eds), *Handbook of Visual Analysis*. London: Sage, pp. 183–204.

Israel, M. and Hay, I. (2006) *Research Ethics for Social Scientists*. London: Sage.

James, W. (1997) 'The names of fear: memory, history, and the ethnography of feeling among Uduk refugees', *Journal of the Royal Anthropological Institute*, 3: 115–31.

Jay, M. (1989) 'In the empire of the gaze', in L. Appignanesi (ed.), *Postmodernism*. London: Free Association Books, pp. 19–25.

Jay, M. (1992) 'Scopic regimes of modernity', in S. Lash and J. Friedman (eds), *Modernity and Identity*. Oxford: Blackwell, pp. 178–95.

Jenkins, R. (1992) *Pierre Bourdieu*. London: Routledge.

Jenks, C. (1995) 'The centrality of the eye in western culture: an introduction', in C. Jenks (ed.), *Visual Culture*. London: Routledge, pp. 1–25.

Jewitt, C. and Oyama, R. (2001) 'Visual meaning: a social semiotic approach', in T. van Leeuwen and C. Jewitt (eds), *Handbook of Visual Analysis*, London: Sage, pp. 134–56.

Jordan, P.-L. (1992) *Cinéma/cinema/kino*. Marseille: Musées de Marseille.

Kingston, D.P. (2003) 'Remembering our namesakes: audience reactions to archival film of King Island, Alaska', in L. Peers and A. Brown (eds), *Museums and Source Communities: A Routledge Reader*. London: Routledge, pp. 123–35.

References

Krebs, S. (1975) 'The film elicitation technique', in P. Hockings (ed.), *Principles of Visual Anthropology*, The Hague: Mouton, pp. 283–301.

Kress, G. and van Leeuwen, T. (1996) *Reading Images: The Grammar of Visual Design*. London: Routledge.

Kuper, A. (1988) *The Invention of Primitive Society: Transformations of an Illusion*. London: Routledge.

Kvale, S. (2007) *Doing Interviews* (Book 2 of *The SAGE Qualitative Research Kit*). London: Sage.

Latour, B. (1988) 'Opening one eye while closing the other ... a note on some religious paintings', in G. Fyfe and J. Law (eds), *Picturing Power: Visual Depiction and Social Relations*, London: Routledge, pp. 15–38.

Latour, B. (1991) 'Technology is society made durable', in J. Law (ed.), *A Sociology of Monsters: Essays on Power, Technology and Domination*. London: Routledge, pp. 103–31.

Leach, E. (1989) 'Tribal ethnography: past, present, future', in E. Tonkin, M. McDonald and M. Chapman (eds), *History and Ethnicity*. London: Routledge, pp. 34–47.

Leslie, J. (1995) 'Digital photopros and photo(shop) realism', *Wired*, 3(5): 108–13.

Lévi-Strauss, C. (1983) *The Way of the Masks*. London: Jonathan Cape.

Lister, M. and Wells, L. (2001) 'Seeing beyond belief: cultural studies as an approach to analysing the visual', in T. van Leeuwen and C. Jewitt (eds), *Handbook of Visual Analysis*. London: Sage, pp. 61–91.

Loizos, P. (1993) *Innovation in Ethnographic Film: From Innocence to Self-Consciousness, 1955–1985*. Manchester: Manchester University Press.

Lomax, A. (1975) 'Audiovisual tools for the analysis of culture style', in P. Hockings (ed.), *Principles of Visual Anthropology*. The Hague: Mouton, pp. 303–24.

Lombroso, C. (1887) *L'homme Criminel*. Paris: F. Alcan.

Lull, J. (1990) *Inside Family Viewing: Ethnographic Research on Television's Audiences*. London: Routledge, for Comedia.

Lutkehaus, N. and Cool, J. (1999) 'Paradigms lost and found: the "crisis of representation" and visual anthropology', in J.M. Gaines and M. Renov (eds), *Collecting Visible Evidence*. Minneapolis: University of Minnesota Press, pp. 116–39.

Lynd, R.S. and Lynd, H.M. (1937) *Middletown in Transition: A Study in Cultural conflicts*. New York: Harcourt, Brace.

MacDougall, D. (1997) 'The visual in anthropology', in M. Banks and H. Morphy (eds), *Rethinking Visual Anthropology*. New Haven: Yale University Press, pp. 276–95.

MacDougall, D. (1998) *Transcultural Cinema*. Princeton: Princeton University Press.

Marcus, G. (1995) 'Ethnography in/of the world system: the emergence of multi-sited ethnography', *Annual Review of Anthropology*, 24: 95–117.

Marcus, G. and Cushman, D. (1982) *Ethnographies as Texts*. Palo Alto, CA: Annual Reviews Inc.

Marcus, G. and Fischer M.M.J. (1986) *Anthropology as Cultural Critique: An Experimental Moment in the Human Sciences*. Chicago: University of Chicago Press.

Martinez, W. (1990) 'Critical studies and visual anthropology: aberrant vs. anticipated readings of ethnographic film', *CVA Review*, Spring: 34–47.

Martinez, W. (1992) 'Who constructs anthropological knowledge? Toward a theory of ethnographic film spectatorship', in P. Crawford and D. Turton (eds), *Film as Ethnography*. Manchester: Manchester University Press, in association with the Granada Centre for Visual Anthropology, pp. 131–61.

Mead, M. (1995 (1975)) 'Visual anthropology in a discipline of words', in P. Hockings (ed.), *Principles of Visual Anthropology* Berlin: Mouton de Gruyter, pp. 3–10.

Meskell, L. and Pels, P. (eds) (2005) *Embedding Ethics*. Oxford: Berg.

References

Michaels, E. (1986) *The Aboriginal Invention of Television in Central Australia, 1982–1986: Report of the Fellowship to Assess the Impact of Television in Remote Aboriginal Communities.* Canberra: Australian Institute of Aboriginal Studies.

Michaels, E. (1991a) 'Aboriginal content: who's got it – who needs it?', *Visual Anthropology*, 4: 277–300.

Michaels, E. (1991b) 'A model of teleported texts (with reference to Aboriginal television)', *Visual Anthropology*, 4: 301–23.

Minh-ha, T.T. (1991) *When the Moon Waxes Red: Representation, Gender and Cultural Politics.* New York: Routledge.

Mirzoeff, N. (1999) *An Introduction to Visual Culture.* London: Routledge.

Mizen, P. (2005) 'A little "light work"? Children's images of their labour', *Visual Studies*, 20: 124–39.

Monmonier, M. (1991) *How to Lie with Maps.* Chicago: University of Chicago Press.

Moore, H.L. (1988) *Feminism and Anthropology.* Cambridge: Polity Press.

Morley, D. (1992) *Television, Audiences and Cultural Studies.* London: Routledge.

Morley, D. (1995) 'Television: not so much a visual medium, more a visible object', in C. Jenks (ed.), *Visual Culture.* London: Rouledge, pp. 170–89.

Morley, D. (1996) 'The audience, the ethnographer, the postmodernist and their problems', in P.I. Crawford and S.B. Hafsteinsson (eds), *The Construction of the Viewer: Proceedings from NAFA 3.* Højbjerg, Denmark: Intervention Press, pp. 11–27.

Morphy, H. and Banks, M. (1997) 'Introduction: rethinking visual anthropology', in M. Banks and H. Morphy (eds), *Rethinking Visual Anthropology.* London: Yale University Press, pp. 1–35.

Mulvey, L. (1975) 'Visual pleasure and narrative cinema', *Screen*, 16: 6–18.

Nichols, B. (1988 (1983)) 'The voice of documentary', in A. Rosenthal (ed.), *New Challenges for Documentary.* Berkeley: University of California Press, pp. 48–63.

Niessen, S. (1991) 'More to it than meets the eye: photo-elicitation among the Batak of Sumatra', *Visual Anthropology*, 4: 415–30.

Peers, L. and Brown, A. (2003) 'Introduction', in L. Peers and A. Brown (eds), *Museums and Source Communities: A Routledge Reader.* London: Routledge, pp. 1–16.

Pink, S. (2001) *Doing Visual Ethnography: Images, Media and Representation in Research.* London: Sage.

Pink, S. (2006) *The Future of Visual Anthropology: Engaging the Senses.* London: Routledge.

Pinney, C. (1992) 'The parallel histories of anthropology and photography', in E. Edwards (ed.), *Anthropology and Photography, 1869–1920.* New Haven, CT: Yale University Press in association with The Royal Anthropological Institute, London, pp. 74–95.

Pinney, C. (1997) *Camera Indica: The Social Life of Indian Photographs.* London: Reaktion Books.

Pinney, C. and Peterson, N. (eds) (2003) *Photography's Other Histories.* Durham, N.C: Duke University Press.

Poignant, R. (1992) 'Surveying the field of view: the making of the RAI photographic collection', in E. Edwards (ed.), *Anthropology and Photography, 1860–1920*, New Haven: Yale University Press, in association with The Royal Anthropological Institute, London, pp. 42–73.

Prost, J.H. (1975) 'Filming body behaviour', in P. Hockings (ed.), *Principles of Visual Anthropology.* The Hague: Mouton, pp. 325–63.

Prosser, J. (1998) 'The status of image-based research', in J. Prosser (ed.), *Image-Based Research: A Sourcebook for Qualitative Researchers.* London: Falmer Press, pp. 97–112.

Prosser, J. (2000) 'The moral maze of image ethics', in H. Simons and R. Usher (eds), *Situated Ethics in Educational Research.* London: Routledge, pp. 116–32.

References

Ramos, M.J. (2004) 'The limitations of intercultural *ekphrasis*', in S. Pink, L. Kürti and A.I. Afonso (eds), *Working Images: Visual Research and Representation in Ethnography*. London: Routledge, pp. 147–59.

Rapley, T. (2007) *Doing Conversation, Discourse and Document Analysis* (Book 7 of *The SAGE Qualitative Research Kit*). London: Sage.

Richardson, J. and Kroeber, A. (1940) 'Three centuries of women's dress fashions: a quantitative analysis', *Anthropological Records*, 5: 111–53.

Robinson, D. (1976) 'Fashions in the shaving and trimming of the beard: the men of the *Illustrated London News*, 1842–1972', *American Journal of Sociology*, 81: 1133–41.

Root, J. (1986) *Open the Box*. London: Comedia Publishing Group.

Rose, G. (2001) *Visual Methodologies: An Introduction to the Interpretation of Visual Materials*. London: Sage.

Rosenthal, A. (ed.) (1980) *The Documentary Conscience: A Casebook in Film Making*. Berkeley: University of California Press.

Rouch, J. (1975) 'The camera and man', in P. Hockings (ed.) *Principles of Visual Anthropology*. The Hague: Mouton, pp. 29–46.

Ruby, J. (2000) *Picturing Culture: Explorations in Film and Anthropology*. Chicago: University of Chicago Press.

Ruby, J. (2005) 'Jean Rouch: hidden and revealed', *American Anthropologist*, 107: 111–12.

Rundstrom, D. (1988) 'Imaging anthropology', in J. Rollwagon (ed.), *Anthropological Filmmaking: Anthropological Perspectives on the Production of Film and Video for the General Public*. Chur: Harwood Academic Press, pp. 317–70.

Schratz, M. and Steiner-Löffler, U. (1998) 'Pupils using photographs in school self-evaluation', in J. Prosser (ed.), *Image Based Research: A Sourcebook for Qualitative Researchers*. London: Falmer Press, pp. 235–51.

Schwartz, D. (1993) 'Superbowl XXVI: reflections on the manufacture of appearance', *Visual Sociology*, 8: 23–33.

Schwartz, J.M. and Ryan, J.R. (eds) (2003) *Picturing Place: Photography and the Geographical Imagination*. London: I.B. Tauris.

Seely, H. (2003) 'The poetry of D.H. Rumsfeld: recent works by the secretary of defense', *Slate*, April, www.slate.com/id/2081042/.

Sharples, M., Davison, L., Thomas, G. and Rudman, P. (2003) 'Children as photographers: an analysis of children's photographic behaviour and intentions at three age levels', *Visual Communication*, 2: 303–30.

Silverstone, R. (1985) *Framing Science: The Making of a BBC Documentary*. London: BFI Books.

Souza, L.M.T.M. de (2002) 'Review of: Jessica Evans and Stuart Hall (eds), *Visual Culture: The Reader*. London: Sage, 1999 and Nicholas Mirzoeff, (ed.), *The Visual Culture Reader*. London: Routledge, 1998, *Visual Communication*, 1: 129 36.

Stanton, J. (2003) 'Snapshots on the dreaming: photographs of the past and present', in L. Peers and A. Brown (eds), *Museums and Source Communities: A Routledge Reader*. London: Routledge, pp. 136–51.

Steiger, R. (1995) 'First children and family dynamics', *Visual Sociology*, 10: 28–49.

Stocking, G. (1982) *Race, Culture and Evolution: Essays on the History of Anthropology*. Chicago: University of Chicago Press.

Stoller, P. (1989) *The Taste of Ethnographic Things: The Senses in Anthropology*. Philadelphia: University of Pennsylvania Press.

Suchar, C. (1997) 'Grounding visual sociology research in shooting scripts', *Qualitative Sociology*, 20: 33–55.

References

SVA (Society for Visual Anthropology) (2001) *Guidelines for the Evaluation of Ethnographic Visual Media.* Society for Visual Anthropology. http.www. society for visual anthropology.org/resources/svaevalution.pdf/

Tagg, J. (1987) *The Burden of Representation: Essays on Photographies and Histories.* London: Macmillan.

ten Have, P. (2004) *Understanding Qualitative Research and Ethnomethodology.* London: Sage.

Trachtenberg, A. (1989) *Reading American Photographs. Images as History: Mathew Brady to Walker Evans.* New York: Noonday Press.

Tufte, E.R. (1997) *Visual Explanations: Images and Quantities, Evidence and Narrative.* Cheshire, CT: Graphics Press.

Turner, T. (1990) 'Visual media, cultural politics and anthropological practice: some implications of recent uses of film and video among the Kayapó of Brazil', *CVA Review,* Spring: 8–12.

Turner, T. (1992) 'Defiant images: the Kayapó appropriation of video', *Anthropology Today,* 8: 5–16.

van der Does, P., Edelaar, S., Gooskens, I., Liefting, M. and van Mierlo, M. (1992) 'Reading images: a study of a Dutch neighborhood', *Visual Sociology,* 7: 4–67.

van Leeuwen, T. (2001) 'Semiotics and iconography', in T. van Leeuwen and C. Jewitt (eds), *Handbook of Visual Analysis.* London: Sage, pp. 92–118.

van Leeuwen, T. and Jewitt, C. (eds) (2001) *Handbook of Visual Analysis.* London: Sage.

van Wezel, R.H.J. (1988) 'Reciprocity of research results in Portugal', *Critique of Anthropology,* 8: 63–70.

Whorf, B.L. (1956) *Language, Thought and Reality.* Cambridge, MA: MIT Press.

Williams, M. (2002) *Making Sense of Social Research.* London: Sage.

Wood, D. (ed.) (2003) *Foucault and Panopticism Revisited,* online at www.surveillance-and-society.org.

Woolgar, S. (1991) 'Configuring the user: the case of usability trials', in J. Law (ed.), *A Sociology of Monsters: Essays on Power, Technology and Domination.* London: Routledge, pp. 57–99.

Worth, S. and Adair, J. (1972) *Through Navajo Eyes: An Exploration in Film Communication and Anthropology.* Bloomington: University Indiana Press.

Worth, S. and Adair, J. (1997) *Through Navajo Eyes: An Exploration in Film Communication and Anthropology with a New Foreword, Afterword, and Illustrations by Richard Chalfen.* Albuquerque: University of New Mexico Press.

Wright, T. (1999) *The Photography Handbook.* London: Routledge.

III Author index

III Subject index